Pharmacokinetics The study of absorption, distribution, metabolism and excretion of drugs.	**What** - Drug biotransformation in the organism- Distribution of drugs in the organism- Excretion of substances
The main mechanism of most drugs absorption in GI tract is Passive diffusion (lipid diffusion)	What kind of substances can't permeate membranes by passive diffusion? Hydrophilic substances
A hydrophilic medicinal agent has the following property Low ability to penetrate through the cell membrane lipids.	What is implied by «active transport»? Transport against concentration gradient
What does the term "bioavailability" mean? Fraction of an uncharged drug reaching the systemic circulation following any route administration.	The reasons determing bioavailability are Extent of absorption and hepatic first-pass effect
Pick out the appropriate alimentary route of administration when passage of drugs through liver is minimized Rectal	Which route of drug administration is most likely to lead to the first-pass effect? Oral

What is characteristic of the oral route? Absorption depends on GI tract secretion and motor function.	**Tick the feature of the sublingual route** Pretty fast absorption
Pick out the parenteral route of medicinal agent administration Inhalation, IV.	**Parenteral administration** Usually produces a more rapid response than oral administration
What is characteristic of the intramuscular route of drug administration? Oily solutions can be injected	**True or False. Intravenous injections are more suitable for oily solutions.** FALSE.
True or False. Intravenous administration provides a rapid response TRUE	**True or False. Intramuscular administration requires a sterile technique** TRUE
True or False. Subcutaneous administration may cause local irritation TRUE	**True or False. Most of drugs are distributed homogeneously.** FALSE

Biological barriers include - Cell membranes - Capillary walls - Placenta	**What is the reason of complicated penetration of some drugs through brain-blood barrier?** Absence of pores in the brain capillary endothelium
The volume of distribution (Vd) relates The amount of a drug in the body to the concentration of a drug in plasma.	**For the calculation of the volume of distribution (Vd) one must take into account** Concentration of a substance in plasma
The term "biotransformation" includes Process of physicochemical and biochemical alteration of a drug in the body.	**Tick the drug type for which microsomal oxidation is the most prominent** Lipid soluble
True or False. Microsomal oxidation results in an increase of ionization and water solubility of a drug TRUE	**Stimulation of liver microsomal enzymes can** Require the dose increase of some drugs.
Metabolic transformation (phase 1) is Transformation of substances due to oxidation, reduction or hydrolysis.	**Biotransformation of a medicinal substance results in** Faster urinary excretion.

Conjugation Coupling of a drug with an endogenous substrate	Which of the following processes proceeds in the second phase of biotransformation Acetylation
Conjugation of a drug includes - Glucoronidation- Sulfate formation- Methylation	True or False. Metabolic transformation and conjugation usually results in an increase of a substance biological activity FALSE
In case of liver disorders accompanied by a decline in microsomal enzyme activity the duration of action of some drugs is Enlarged	Half life (t ½) is the time required to Change the amount of a drug in plasma by half during elimination.
Half life (t ½) doesn't depend on Time of drug absorption	Half life (t ½) depends on - Biotransformation- Concentration of a drug in plasma- Rate of drug elimination
Elimination is expressed as Clearance of an organism from a xenobiotic.	Elimination rate constant (Kelim) is defined by the following parameter Half life (t ½)

True or False. The most rapid eliminated drugs are those with high glomerular filtration rate and actively secreted but aren't passively reabsorbed TRUE	**Systemic clearance (CLs) is related with** Volume of distribution, half life and elimination rate constant.
Pharmacodynamics involves the study of - Biological and therapeutic effects of drugs- Mechanisms of drug action- Drug interactions- Information about unwanted effects	**The most appropriate to the term "receptor"** Active macromolecular components of a cell or an organism which a drug molecule has to combine with in order to elicit its specific effect
What does "affinity" mean A measure of how tightly a drug binds to a receptor	**Target proteins which a drug molecule binds are** - Only receptors- Only ion channels- Only carriers
An agonist is a substance that Interacts with the receptor and initiates changes in cell function, producing various effects	**If an agonist can produce maximal effects and has high efficacy it's called** Full agonist
If an agonist can produce submaximal effects and has moderate efficacy it's called Partial agonist	**An antagonist is a substance that** Binds to the receptors without directly altering their functions

A competitive antagonist is a substance that Binds to the same receptor site and progressively inhibits the agonist response	The substance binding to one receptor subtype as an agonist and to another as an antagonist is called Agonist-antagonist
Irreversible interaction of an antagonist with a receptor is due to Covalent bonds	Tick the second messenger of G-protein-coupled (metabotropic) receptor cAMP
Tick the substance which changes the activity of an effector element but doesn't belong to second messengers G–protein	The increase of second messengers' (cAMP, cGMP, Ca^{2+} etc.) concentration leads to Proteinkinases activation and protein phosphorylation.
Tick the substances whose mechanisms are based on interaction with ion channels - Sodium channel blockers- Calcium channel blockers- Potassium channels activators	Efficacy is the maximum effect of a drug
Potency is a comparative measure, refers to the different doses of two drugs that are needed to produce the same effect	Therapeutical dose The amount of a substance to produce the required effect in most patients

Toxic dose The amount of substance to produce effects hazardous for an organism	Which effect may lead to toxic reactions when a drug is taken continuously or repeatedly Cumulative effect
What term is used to describe a more gradual decrease in responsiveness to a drug, taking days or weeks to develop? Tolerance	What term is used to describe a decrease in responsiveness to a drug which develops in a few minutes? Tachyphylaxis
Tachyphylaxis Very rapidly developing tolerance	True or False. Drug resistance is a term used to describe the loss of effectiveness of antimicrobial or antitumour drugs. TRUE
Tolerance and drug resistance can be a consequence of - Increased metabolic degradation - Change in receptors, loss of them or exhaustion of mediators -	True or False. Dependence is often associated with tolerance to a drug, a physical abstinence syndrome, and psychological dependence (craving). TRUE
The situation when failure to continue administering the drug results in serious psychological and somatic disturbances is called? Abstinence syndrome	What is the type of drug-to-drug interaction which is connected with processes of absorption, biotransformation, distribution and excretion? Pharmacokinetic interaction

What is the type of drug-to-drug interaction which is the result of interaction at receptor, cell, enzyme or organ level? Pharmacodynamic interaction	**What phenomenon can occur in case of using a combination of drugs?** Synergism
If two drugs with the same effect, taken together, produce an effect that is equal in magnitude to the sum of the effects of the drugs given individually, it is called as Additive effect	**What does the term "potentiation" mean?** Intensive increase of drug effects due to their combination
The types of antagonism are Competitive	**The term "chemical antagonism" means that** Two drugs combine with one another to form an inactive compound
A teratogenic action is Negative action on the fetus causing fetal malformation	**Characteristic unwanted reaction which isn't related to a dose or to a pharmacodynamic property of a drug is called** Hypersensitivity
Idiosyncratic reaction of a drug is Unpredictable, inherent, qualitatively abnormal reaction to a drug	**Therapeutic index (TI) is** A ratio used to evaluate the safety and usefulness of a drug for indication

Local anesthetics produce Blocking pain sensation without loss of consciousness	**A good local anesthetic agent shouldn't cause** Fast onset and long duration of action
Most local anesthetic agents consist of - Lipophylic group (frequently an aromatic ring)- Intermediate chain (commonly including an ester or amide)- Amino group	**Which one of the following groups is responsible for the duration of the local anesthetic action?** Intermediate chain
Indicate the local anesthetic agent, which has a shorter duration of action Procaine	**Which one of the following groups is responsible for the potency and the toxicity of local anesthetics?** Lipophylic group
Indicate the drug, which has greater potency of the local anesthetic action Bupivacaine	**Ionizable group is responsible for** The ability to diffuse to the site of action
Which one of the following local anesthetics is an ester of benzoic acid? Cocaine	**Indicate the local anesthetic, which is an ester of paraaminobenzoic acid** Procaine

Which of the following local anesthetics is an acetanilide derivative? Lidocaine	**Indicate the local anesthetic, which is a toluidine derivative** Prilocaine
Which of the following local anesthetics is a thiophene derivative? Ultracaine	**Local anesthetics are** Weak bases
For therapeutic application local anesthetics are usually made available as salts for the reasons of More stability and greater water solubility	**Which of the following statements is not correct for local anesthetics?** charged cationic form penetrates biologic membranes more readily than an uncharged form
Which one of the following statements about the metabolism of local anesthetics is incorrect? Metabolism of local anesthetics occurs at the site of administration	**Indicate the anesthetic agent of choice in patient with a liver disease** Procaine
Which of the following local anesthetics is preferable in patient with pseudocholinesterase deficiency? Ropivacaine	**The primary mechanism of action of local anesthetics is** Blockade of voltage-gated sodium channels

A local anesthetics that is water-soluble Procaine	**Indicate the local anesthetic, which is more lipid-soluble** Bupivacaine
The more lipophylic drugs - Are more potent- Have longer duration of action- Bind more extensively to proteins	**Which fibers is the first to be blocked?** B and C fibers
The function, which the last to be blocked: Motor function	**Which of the following fibers participates in high-frequency pain transmission?** Type A delta and C fibers
Local anesthetics that is an useful antiarrhythmic agent? Lidocaine	**Indicate the route of local anesthetic administration, which is associated with instillation within epidural or subarachnoid spaces** Spinal anesthesia
The choice of a local anesthetic for specific procedures is usually based on - The duration of action- Water solubility- Capability of rapid penetration through the skin or mucosa with limited tendency to diffuse away from the site of application	**What anesthetics has a short-acting drug?** Procaine

Indicate the local anesthetic, which is a long-acting agent Bupivacaine	**The anesthetic effect of the agents of short and intermediate duration of action can not be prolonged by adding** Dopamine
A vasoconstrictor does not Reduce a local anesthetic uptake by the nerve	**A vasoconstrictor does** - Retard the removal of drug from the injection site- Hence the chance of toxicity- Decrease the blood level
Vasoconstrictors are less effective in prolonging anesthetic properties of Bupivacaine	**Which of the following local anesthetics is only used for surface or topical anesthesia?** Cocaine
Indicate the local anesthetic, which is mainly used for regional nerve block anesthesia Bupivacaine	**Which local anesthetics is used for infiltrative and regional anesthesia?** - Procaine- Lidocaine- Mepivacaine
Indicate the local anesthetic, which is used for spinal anesthesia Tetracaine	**Which local anesthetics is called a universal anesthetic?** Lidocaine

Most serious toxic reaction to local anesthetics is - Seizures - Cardiovascular collapse - Respiratory failure	**Correct statements concerning cocaine include** - Cocaine is often used for nose and throat procedures - Limited use because of abuse potential - Causes sympathetically mediated tachycardia and vasoconstriction
Which local anesthetics is more cardiotoxic? Bupivacaine	**Most local anesthetics can cause** - Depression of abnormal cardiac pacemaker activity, excitability, conduction - Depression of the strength of cardiac contraction - Cardiovascular collapse
Which local anesthetics causes methemoglobinemia? Prilocaine	**Procaine has all of the following propertie** - It has ester linkage - Its metabolic product can inhibit the action of sulfonamides - It is relatively short-acting
Procaine has all of the following properties EXCEPT It readily penetrates the skin and mucosa	**Correct statements concerning lidocaine include** - It is an universal anesthetic - It widely used as an antiarrhythmic agent - It is metabolized in liver
Correct statements concerning lidocaine include all of the following EXCEPT It has esteratic linkage	**Which local anesthetics is more likely to cause allergic reactions?** Procaine

Tetracaine has all of the following properties	Tetracaine has all of the following properties EXCEPT
- Slow onset- Long duration- High toxicity	Low potency
Correct statements concerning bupivacaine include	Correct statements concerning bupivacaine include all of the following EXCEPT
- It has amide linkage- It is a long-acting drug- An intravenous injection can lead to seizures	It has low cardiotoxicity
Acetylcholine is not a specific neurotransmitter at	Acetylcholine is a specific neurotransmitter at
Sympathetic postganglionic nerve endings	- Sympathetic ganglia- Parasympathetic ganglia- Parasympathetic postganglionic nerve endings
Muscarinic receptors are located in	Indicate the location of M2 cholinoreceptor type
Autonomic effector cells	Heart
The symptoms of mushroom poisoning include	The symptoms of mushroom poisoning include all of the following EXCEPT
- Salivation, lacrimation, nausea, vomiting- Headache, abdominal colic- Bradycardia, hypotension and shock	Dryness of mouth, hyperpyrexia, hallucination

Which cholinomimetics activates both muscarinic and nicotinic receptors? Bethanechol	Indicate a cholinomimetic agent, which is related to direct-acting drugs Carbachol
Characteristics of carbachol include - It decreases intraocular pressure- It exerts both nicotinic and muscarinic effects- It is resistant to acethylcholiesterase	Characteristics of carbachol include all of the following EXCEPT It causes mydriasis
Acetylcholine is not used in clinical practice because It is very rapidly hydrolyzed.	Parasympathomimetic drugs cause Bradycardia
Which direct-acting cholinomimetics is mainly muscarinic in action? Bethanechol	Which direct-acting cholinomimetics has the shortest duration of action? Acetylcholine
Bethanechol has all of the following properties - It is extremely resistant to hydrolysis- Purely muscarinic in its action- It is used for abdominal urinary bladder distention	Bethanechol has all of the following properties EXCEPT It exerts both nicotinic and muscarinic effects

Q	A
A M-cholinimimetic agent is	Pilocarpine
Characteristics of pilocarpine include	- It is a tertiary amine alkaloid- It causes miosis and a decrease in intraocular pressure- It is useful in the treatment of glaucoma
Characteristics of pilocarpine include all of the following EXCEPT	Causes a decrease in secretory and motor activity of gut
Which cholinomimetics is a plant derivative with lower potency than nicotine but with a similar spectrum of action?	Lobeline
Which cholinomimetics is indirect-acting?	Edrophonium
The mechanism of action of indirect-acting cholinomimetic agents is	Inhibition of the hydrolysis of endogenous acetylcholine
Indicate a reversible cholinesterase inhibitor	Physostigmine
Which cholinesterase inhibitors is irreversible?	Isoflurophate
Indicate cholinesterase activator	Pralidoxime
Isofluorophate increases all of the following effects except	Bronchodilation

Isofluorophate increases all of the following effects - Lacrimation- Muscle twitching- Salivation	**Indicate a cholinesterase inhibitor, which has an additional direct nicotinic agonist effect** Neostigmine
Cholinesterase inhibitors do not produce Dramatic hypertension and tachycardia	**Which cholinomimetics is commonly used in the treatment of glaucoma?** Pilocarpine
Indicate the organophosphate cholinesterase inhibitor, which can be made up in an aqueous solution for ophthalmic use and retains its activity within a week: Echothiophate	**Which cholinomimetics is most widely used for paralytic ileus and atony of the urinary bladder?** Neostigmine
Chronic long-term therapy of myasthenia is usually accomplished with Neostigmine	**Which cholinomimetics is a drug of choice for reversing the effects of nondepolarizing neuromuscular relaxants?** Edrophonium
Indicate the reversible cholinesterase inhibitor, which penetrates the blood-brain bar Physostigmine	**Which cholinomimetics is used in the treatment of atropine intoxication?** Physostigmine

The symptoms of excessive stimulation of muscarinic receptors include - Abdominal cramps, diarrhea- Increased salivation, excessive bronchial secretion- Miosis, bradycardia	**The symptoms of excessive stimulation of muscarinic receptors include all of the following EXCEPT** Weakness of all skeletal muscles
The excessive stimulation of muscarinic receptors by pilocarpine and choline esters is blocked competitively by: Atropine	**The toxic effects of a large dose of nicotine include** - Convulsions, coma and respiratory arrest- Skeletal muscle depolarization blockade and respiratory paralysis- Hypertension and cardiac arrhythmias
The toxic effects of a large dose of nicotine include all of the following EXCEPT Hypotension and bradycardia	**The dominant initial sights of acute cholinesterase inhibitors intoxication include** - Salivation, sweating- Bronchial constriction- Vomiting and diarrhea
The dominant initial sights of acute cholinesterase inhibitors intoxication include all of the following except Mydriasis	**Which drugs is used for acute toxic effects of organophosphate cholinesterase inhibitors?** Pralidoxime
The group of nicotinic receptor-blocking drugs consists of - Ganglion-blockers- Neuromuscular junction blockers	**M3 receptor subtype is located** On effector cell membranes of glandular and smooth muscle cells

Which drugs is both a muscarinic and nicotinic blocker?	Benztropine
Indicate a muscarinic receptor-blocking drug	Scopolamine
Which agents is a ganglion-blocking drug?	Hexamethonium
Indicate the skeletal muscle relaxant, which is a depolarizing agent	Succinylcholine
Which drugs is a nondepolarizing muscle relaxant?	Pancuronium
Indicate the drug, which is rapidly and fully distributed into CNS and has a greater effect than most other antimuscarinic agents?	Scopolamine
The effect of the drug on parasympathetic function declines rapidly in	- Heart - Smooth muscle organs - Glands
The effect of the drug on parasympathetic function declines rapidly in all organs EXCEPT	Eye
The mechanism of atropine action is	Competitive muscarinic blockade
The tissues most sensitive to atropine are	The salivary, bronchial and sweat glands

Atropine is highly selective for - M1 receptor subtype- M2 receptor subtype- M3 receptor subtype	**Which antimuscarinic drugs is often effective in preventing or reversing vestibular disturbances, especially motion sickness?** Scopolamine
Atropine causes Mydriasis, a rise in intraocular pressure and cyclo	**Patients complain of dry or "sandy" eyes when receiving large doses of** Atropine
All of the following parts of the heart are very sensitive to muscarinic receptor blockade - Atria- Sinoatrial node- Atrioventricular node	**All of the following parts of the heart are very sensitive to muscarinic receptor blockade except:** Ventricle
Atropine causes Tachycardia, little effect on blood pressure and bronchodilation	**Atropine is frequently used prior to administration of inhalant anesthetics to reduce** Secretions
Atropine is now rarely used for the treatment of peptic ulcer because of - Slow gastric empting and prolongation of the exposure of the ulcer bed to acid- Low efficiency and necessity of large doses- Adverse effects	**Which antimuscarinic drugs is a selective M1 blocker?** Pirenzepine

Atropine causes Spasmolitic activity	**Which drugs is useful in the treatment of uterine spasms?** Atropine
Atropine may cause a rise in body temperature (atropine fever) In infants and children	**The pharmacologic actions of scopolamine most closely resemble those of** Atropine
Compared with atropine, scopolamine has all of the following properties - More marked central effect- More potent in producing mydriasis and cycloplegia- Lower effects on the heart, bronchial muscle and intestines	**Compared with atropine, scopolamine has all of the following properties EXCEPT** Less potent in decreasing bronchial, salivary and sweat gland secretion
Which drugs is useful in the treatment of Parkinson's disease? Benztropine	**Indicate the antimuscarinic drug, which is used as a mydriatic** Homatropine
Which agents is used as an inhalation drug in asthma? Ipratropium	**Which agents is most effective in regenerating cholinesterase associated with skeletal muscle neuromuscular junctions?** Pralidoxime

Indicate an antimuscarinic drug, which is effective in the treatment of mushroom poising	Antimuscarinics are used in the treatment of
Atropine	- Motion sickness - Hyperhidrosis - Asthma
Antimuscarinics are used in the treatment of the following disorders EXCEPT	The atropine poisoning includes all of the following symptoms EXCEPT
Glaucoma	Bradicardia, orthostatic hypotension
The atropine poisoning includes all of the following symptoms	The treatment of the antimuscarinic effects can be carried out with
- Mydriasis, cycloplegia - Hyperthermia, dry mouth, hot and flushed skin - Agitation and delirium	Neostigmine
Contraindications to the use of antimuscarinic drugs are	Contraindications to the use of antimuscarinic drugs are all of the following except
- Glaucoma - Myasthenia - Paralytic ileus and atony of the urinary bladder	Bronchial asthma
Hexamethonium blocks the action of acetylcholine and similar agonists at	The applications of the ganglion blockers have disappeared because of all of the following reasons EXCEPT
Autonomic ganglia	Respiratory depression

The applications of the ganglion blockers have disappeared because of all of the following reasons - Orthostatic hypotension- Lack of selectivity- Homeostatic reflexes block	**Which agents is a short-acting ganglion blocker?** Trimethaphane
Indicate the ganglion-blocking drug, which can be taken orally for the treatment of hypertension? Mecamylamine	**The systemic effects of hexamethonium include** - Reduction of both peripheral vascular resistance and venous return- Partial mydriasis and loss of accommodation- Constipation and urinary retention
The systemic effects of hexamethonium include all of the following EXCEPT Stimulation of thermoregulatory sweating	**Ganglion blocking drugs are used for the following emergencies** - Hypertensive crises- Controlled hypotension- Pulmonary edema
Ganglion blocking drugs are used for the following emergencies EXCEPT Cardiovascular collapse	**Agents that produce neuromuscular blockade act by inhibiting:** Interaction of acetylcholine with cholinergic receptors
Skeletal muscle relaxation and paralysis can occur from interruption of functions at several sites, including - Nicotinic acetylcholine receptors- The motor end plate- Contractile apparatus	**Skeletal muscle relaxation and paralysis can occur from interruption of functions at several sites, including all of the following EXCEPT** Muscarinic acetylcholine receptors

Nondepolarisation neuromuscular blocking agents Prevent access of the transmitter to its receptor and depolarization	**Which drugs has "double-acetylcholine" structure?** Succylcholine
Indicate the long-acting neuromuscular blocking agent Tubocurarine	**Which neuromuscular blocking drugs is an intermediate-duration muscle relaxant?** Vecuronium
Indicate the nondepolarizing agent, which has the fastest onset of effect? Rapacuronium	**Indicate the neuromuscular blocker, whose breakdown product readily crosses the blood-brain barrier and may cause seizures** Atracurium
Which competitive neuromuscular blocking agent could be used in patients with renal failure? Atracurium	**Indicate the nondepolarizing agent, which has short duration of action** Mivacurium
Which depolarizing agent has the extremely brief duration of action? Succinylcholine	**Neuromuscular blockade by both succinylcholine and mivacurium may be prolonged in patients wit** - An abnormal variant of plasma cholinesterase- Hepatic disease

Depolarizing agents include all of the following properties EXCEPT	Interact with nicotinic receptor to compete with acetylcholine without receptor activation
Which neuromuscular blockers causes transient muscle fasciculations?	Succinylcholine
Indicate muscles, which are more resistant to block and recover more rapidly	Diaphragm
Which neuromuscular blocking agent has the potential to cause the greatest release of histamine?	Tubocurarine
Which of the following muscular relaxants causes hypotension and bronchospasm?	Tubocurarine
Indicate the neuromuscular blocker, which causes tachycardia	Pancuronium
Which neuromuscular blocking agents cause cardiac arrhythmias?	Succinylcholine
Effects seen only with depolarizing blockade include	- Hypercaliemia - Emesis - Muscle pain
Effects seen only with depolarizing blockade include all of the following EXCEPT	A decrease in intraocular pressure
Which neuromuscular blocking agent is contraindicated in patients with glaucoma?	Succinylcholine

Indicate the following neuromuscular blocker, which would be contraindicated in patients with renal failure Pipecuronium	All of the following drugs increase the effects of depolarizing neuromuscular blocking agents EXCEPT Nondepolarizing blockers
Drugs that increase the effects of depolarizing neuromuscular blocking agents - Aminoglycosides- Antiarrhythmic drugs- Local anesthetics	Which diseases can augment the neuromuscular blockade produced by nondepolarizing muscle relaxants? Myasthenia gravis
Indicate the agent, which effectively antagonizes the neuromuscular blockade caused by nondepolarizing drugs Neostigmine	Sympathetic stimulation is mediated by - Release of norepinephrine from nerve terminals- Activation of adrenoreceptors on postsynaptic sites- Release of epinephrine from the adrenal medulla
Characteristics of epinephrine include - It is synthesized into the adrenal medulla- It is transported in the blood to target tissues- It directly interacts with and activates adrenoreceptors	Characteristics of epinephrine include all of the following EXCEPT It is synthesized into the nerve ending
Which of the following sympathomimetics acts indirectly? Ephedrine	Indirect action includes all of the following properties EXCEPT Interaction with adrenoreceptors

Catecholamine includes - Epinephrine- Isoprenaline- Norepinephrine	Epinephrine decreases intracellular camp levels by acting on α2 receptor
True or False. Skeletal muscle vessels have predominantly alfa receptors and constrict in the presence of epinephrine and norepinephrine FALSE	True or False. ALFA receptors increase arterial resistence, whereas beta2 receptor promote smooth muscle relaxation TRUE
True or False. The skin and splanchic vessels have predominantly alfa receptors. TRUE	True or False. Vessels in a skeletal muscle may constrict or dilate depending on whether alfa or beta2 receptors are activated TRUE
Direct effects on the heart are determined largely by Beta1 receptor	Which of the following effects is related to direct beta1 adrenoreceptor stimulation? Tachycardia
Distribution of alfa adrenoreceptor subtypes is associated with all of the following tissues - Blood vessels- Prostate- Pupillary dilator muscle	Distribution of alfa adrenoreceptor subtypes is not associated with the tissues of HEART

Beta adrenoreceptor subtypes is not contained in tissues of Pupillary dilator muscle	**Beta adrenoreceptor subtypes is contained in** - Bronchial muscles - Heart - Fat cells
In which tissues both alfa and beta1 adrenergic stimulation produces the same effect? Intestine	**The effects of sympathomimetics on blood pressure are associated with their effects on** - The heart - The peripheral resistance - The venous return
A relatively pure alfa agonist causes - Increase peripheral arterial resistance - Increase venous return - Reflex bradycardia	**A relatively pure alfa agonist do not causes** Effect on blood vessels
A nonselective beta receptor agonist causes - Increase cardiac output - Decrease peripheral arterial resistance - Decrease the mean pressure	**A nonselective beta receptor agonist do not causes** Increase peripheral arterial resistance
True or False. Alfa agonists cause miosis. FALSE	**True or False. Alfa agonists cause mydriasis.** TRUE

True or False. Beta antagonists decrease the production of aqueous humor TRUE	**True or False. Alfa agonists increase the outflow of aqueous humor from the eye** TRUE
A bronchial smooth muscle contains Beta 2 receptor	**All of the following agents are beta receptor agonists** - Epinephrine - Isoproterenol - Dobutamine
All of the following agents are beta receptor agonists EXCEPT Methoxamine	**Which of the following drugs causes bronchodilation without significant cardiac stimulation?** Terbutaline
Alfa-receptor stimulation includes - Relaxation of gastrointestinal smooth muscle - Contraction of bladder base, uterus and prostate - Stimulation of platelet aggregation	**Alfa-receptor stimulation do not includes** Stimulation of insulin secretion
Beta1 receptor stimulation includes - Increase in contractility - Tachycardia - Increase in conduction velocity in the atrioventricular node	**Beta1 receptor stimulation do not includes** Bronchodilation

Beta2 receptor stimulation includes - Stimulation of renin secretion- Fall of potassium concentration in plasma- Relaxation of bladder, uterus	**Beta2 receptor stimulation do not includes** Tachycardia
Hyperglycemia induced by epinephrine is due to - Gluconeogenesis (beta2)- Inhibition of insulin secretion (alfa)- Stimulation of glycogenolysis (beta2)	**Which of the following effects is associated with beta3-receptor stimulation?** Lipolysis
True or False. Norepinephrine has a predominantly beta action FALSE	**True or False. Epinephrine acts on both alfa- and beta-receptors** TRUE
True or False. Methoxamine has a predominantly alfa action TRUE	**True or False. Isoprenaline has a predominantly beta action** TRUE
Indicate the drug, which is a direct-acting both alfa- and beta-receptor agonist Norepinephrine	**Which of the following agents is an alfa1 alfa2 beta1 beta2 receptor agonist?** Epinephrine

Question	Answer
Indicate the direct-acting sympathomimetic, which is an alfa1 alfa2 beta1 receptor agonist	Norepinephrine
Which of the following agents is an alfa1-selective agonist?	Methoxamine
Indicate the alfa2-selective agonist	Xylometazoline
Which agents is a nonselective beta receptor agonist?	Isoproterenol
Indicate the beta1-selective agonist	Dobutamine
Which sympathomimetics is a beta2-selective agonist?	Terbutaline
Indicate the indirect-acting sympathomimetic agent	Ephedrine
Epinephrine produces all of the following effects	- Positive inotropic and chronotropic actions on the heart (beta1 receptor) - Increase peripheral resistance (alfa receptor) - Skeletal muscle blood vessel dilatation (beta2 receptor)
Epinephrine produces all of the following effects EXCEPT	Predominance of alfa effects at low concentration
Epinephrine produces all of the following effects	- Bronchodilation - Hyperglycemia - Mydriasis

Epinephrine produces all of the following effects EXCEPT Decrease in oxygen consumption	**Epinephrine is used in the treatment of** - Bronchospasm- Anaphylactic shock- Open-angle glaucoma
Epinephrine is not used in the treatment of Cardiac arrhythmias	**Compared with epinephrine, norepinephrine do not produces** Decrease the mean pressure below normal before returning to the control value
Norepinephrine produces Vasoconstriction	**Which direct-acting drugs is a relatively pure alfa agonist, an effective mydriatic and decongestant and can be used to raise blood pressure?** Phenylephrine
Characteristics of methoxamine include - It is a direct-acting alfa1-receptor agonist- It causes reflex bradycardia- It increases total peripheral resistance	**Characteristics of methoxamine do not** It increases heart rate, contractility and cardiac output
Which agents is an alfa2-selective agonist with ability to promote constriction of the nasal mucosa? Xylometazoline	**Indicate the sympathomimetic, which may cause hypotension, presumably because of a clonidine-like effect** Xylometazoline

Isoproterenol is Nonselective beta receptor agonist	**Isoproterenol produces** - Increase in cardiac output- Fall in diastolic and mean arterial pressure- Tachycardia
Isoproterenol do not produces Bronchoconstriction	**Characteristics of dobutamine is not** It is used to treat bronchospasm
Characteristics of dobutamine include - It is a relatively beta1-selective synthetic catecholamine- It increases atrioventricular conduction- It causes minimal changes in heart rate and systolic pressure	**Characteristics of salmeterol include** - It is a potent selective beta2 agonist- It causes uterine relaxation- It is used in the therapy of asthma
Characteristics of salmeterol do not include It stimulates heart rate, contractility and cardiac output	**Characteristics of ephedrine include** - It acts primarily through the release of stored cathecholamines- It is a mild CNS stimulant- It causes tachyphylaxis with repeated administration
Characteristics of ephedrine do not include It decreases arterial pressure	**Ephedrine causes** Bronchodilation

Compared with epinephrine, ephedrine produces - It has oral activity - It is resistant to MAO and has much longer duration of action - Its effects are similar, but it is less potent	**Compared with epinephrine, ephedrine do not produces** It is a direct-acting sympathomimetic
Which sympathomimetics is preferable for the treatment of chronic orthostatic hypotension? Ephedrine	**Indicate the sympathomimetic drug, which is used in a hypotensive emergency** Phenylephrine
Which sympathomimetics is preferable for the emergency therapy of cardiogenic shock? Dobutamine	**Indicate the sympathomimetic agent, which is combined with a local anesthetic to prolong the duration of infiltration nerve block** Epinephrine
Which sympathomimetics is related to short-acting topical decongestant agents? Phenylephrine	**Indicate the long-acting topical decongestant agents** Xylometazoline
Which topical decongestant agents is an alfa2-selective agonist? Xylometazoline	**Indicate the sympathomimetic, which may be useful in the emergency management of cardiac arrest** Epinephrine

Which sympathomimetics is used in the therapy of bronchial asthma? Formoterol	**Indicate the agent of choice in the emergency therapy of anaphylactic shock** Epinephrine
Which sympathomimetics is an effective mydriatic? Phenylephrine	**The adverse effects of sympathomimetics include** - Cerebral hemorrhage or pulmonary edema- Myocardial infarction- Ventricular arrhythmias
The adverse effects of sympathomimetics do not include Drug-induced parkinsonism	**Which drugs is a nonselective alfa receptor antagonist?** Phentolamine
Indicate the alfa1-selective antagonist Prazosin	**Which agents is an alfa2–selective antagonist?** Yohimbine
Indicate the irreversible alfa receptor antagonist Phenoxybenzamine	**Which drugs is an nonselective beta receptor antagonist?** Propranolol

Indicate the beta1-selective antagonist Metoprolol	**Which of the following agents is a beta2-selective antagonist?** Butoxamine
Indicate the beta adrenoreceptor antagonist, which has partial beta-agonist activity Pindolol	**Which drugs is a reversible nonselective alfa, beta antagonist?** Labetalol
Indicate the indirect-acting adrenoreceptor blocking drug Reserpine	**The principal mechanism of action of adrenoreceptor antagonists is** Reversible or irreversible interaction with adrenoreceptors
Characteristics of alfa-receptor antagonists do not include Bronchospasm	**Which drugs is an imidazoline derivative and a potent competitive antagonist at both alfa1 and alfa2 receptors?** Phentolamine
Characteristics of phentolamine include - Reduction in peripheral resistance- Tachycardia- Stimulation of muscarinic, H1 and H2 histamine receptors	**Characteristics of phentolamine do not include** Stimulation of responses to serotonin

The principal mechanism of phentolamine-induced tachycardia is Antagonism of presynaptic alfa2 receptors enhances norepinephrine release, which causes cardiac stimulation via unblocked beta receptors	**Nonselective alfa-receptor antagonists are most useful in the treatment of** Pheochromocytoma
The main reason for using alfa-receptor antagonists in the management of pheochromocytoma is Blockade of alfa2 receptors on vascular smooth muscle results in epinephrine stimulation of unblocked alfa2 receptors	**Which drugs is useful in the treatment of pheochromocytoma?** Phentolamine
Indicate adrenoreceptor antagonist agents, which are used for the management of pheochromocytoma Alfa-receptor antagonists	**The principal adverse effects of phentolamine include** - Diarrhea - Arrhythmias - Myocardial ischemia
The principal adverse effects of phentolamine do not include Bradycardia	**Indicate the reversible nonselective alfa-receptor antagonist, which is an ergot derivative** Ergotamine
Indicate an alfa-receptor antagonist, which binds covalently to alfa receptors, causing irreversible blockade of long duration (14-48 hours or longer) Phenoxybenzamine	**Compared with phentolamine, prazosin has all of the following features** - Highly selective for alfa1 receptors - The relative absence of tachycardia - Persistent block of alfa1 receptors

Compared with phentolamine, prazosin has not features Irreversible blockade of alfa receptors	True or False. ALFA1a subtype mediates both vascular and prostate smooth muscle contraction FALSE
True or False. There are at least three subtypes of alfa1 receptors, designated alfa1a, alfa1b and alfa1d TRUE	True or False. ALFA1a subtype mediates prostate smooth muscle contraction TRUE
True or False. ALFA1b subtype mediates vascular smooth muscle contraction TRUE	Indicate an alfa1 adrenoreceptor antagonist, which has great selectivity for alfa1a subtype Tamsulosin
Subtype-selective alfa1 receptor antagonists such as tamsulosin, terazosin, alfusosin are efficacious in Benign prostatic hyperplasia (BPH)	Indicate an alfa receptor antagonist, which is an efficacious drug in the treatment of mild to moderate systemic hypertension Prazosin
Beta-blocking drugs-induced chronically lower blood pressure may be associated with theirs effects on - The heart- The blood vessels- The renin-angiotensin system	Characteristics of beta-blocking agents do not include They induce depression and depleted stores of catecholamines

Beta-receptor antagonists have all of the following cardiovascular effects - The negative inotropic and chronotropic effects - Vasoconstriction - Reduction of the release of renin	**Beta-receptor antagonists have not the following cardiovascular effects** Acute effects of these drugs include a fall in peripheral resistance
Beta-blocking agents have all of the following effects - Bronchoconstriction - Decrease of aqueous humor prodaction - "membrane-stabilizing" action	**Beta-blocking agents have all of the following effects except** Increase plasma concentrations of HDL and decrease of VLDL
Beta-receptor antagonists cause Inhibition of glycogenolysis	**Propranolol has all of the following cardiovascular effects** - It decreases cardiac work and oxygen demand - It inhibits the renin secretion - It increases the atrioventricular nodal refractory period
Propranolol has all of the following cardiovascular effects except It reduces blood flow to the brain	**Propranolol-induced adverse effects include** - Bronchoconstriction - "supersensitivity" of beta-adrenergic receptors (rapid withdrawal) - Sedation, sleep disturbances, depression and sexual dysfunction
Propranolol-induced adverse effects do not include Hyperglycemia	**Propranolol is used in the treatment all of the following diseases** - Cardiovascular diseases - Hyperthyroidism - Migraine headache

Propranolol is used in the treatment all of the following diseases except	Bronchial asthma
Metoprolol and atenolol are members of	The beta1-selective group
Which beta receptor antagonists is preferable in patients with asthma, diabetes or peripheral vascular diseases?	Metoprolol
Indicate a beta receptor antagonist, which has very long duration of action	Nadolol
Indicate a beta1-selective receptor antagonist, which has very long duration of action	Betaxolol
Which drugs is a nonselective beta-blocker without intrinsic sympathomimetic or local anesthetic activity and used for the treatment of life-threatening ventricular arrhythmias?	Sotalol
Indicate a beta receptor antagonist with intrinsic sympathomimetic activity	Oxprenolol
Pindolol, oxprenolol have all of the following properties	- They are nonselective beta antagonists - They are less likely to cause bradycardia and abnormalities in plasma lipids - They are effective in hypertension and angina
Which drugs has both alfa1-selective and beta-blocking effects?	Labetalol
Characteristics of carvedilol include	- It has both alfa1-selective and beta-blocking effects - It attenuates oxygen free radical-initiated lipid peroxidation - It inhibits vascular smooth muscle mitogenesis

Characteristics of carvedilol do not include It is a beta1-selective antagonist	**Indicate the adrenoreceptor antagonist drug, which is a rauwolfia alkaloid** Reserpine
Characteristics of reserpine do not include It inhibits the uptake of norepinephrine into vesicles and MAO	**Indicate a beta-blocker, which is particularly efficacious in thyroid storm** Propranolol
Beta-receptor blocking drugs are used in the treatment all of the following diseases - Hypertension, ischemic heart disease, cardiac arrhythmias- Glaucoma- Hyperthyroidism	**Beta-receptor blocking drugs are used in the treatment all of the following diseases except** Pheochromocytoma
Beta-blocker-induced adverse effects include - Bronchoconstriction- Depression of myocardial contractility and excitability- "supersensitivity" of beta-receptors associated with rapid withdrawal of drugs	**Beta-blocker-induced adverse effects do not include** Hyperglycemia
Hypnotic drugs are used to treat Sleep disorders	**Hypnotic drugs should** Produce drowsiness, encourage the onset and maintenance of sleep

Which chemical agents are used in the treatment of insomnia? - Benzodiazepines- Imidazopyridines- Barbiturates	**Select a hypnotic drug, which is a benzodiazepine derivative** Flurazepam
Tick a hypnotic agent – a barbituric acid derivative Thyopental	**Select a hypnotic drug, which is an imidazopyridine derivative** Zolpidem
Which hypnotic agents is absorbed slowly? Temazepam	**Which barbiturates is an ultra-short-acting drug?** Thiopental
Indicate the barbituric acid derivative, which has 4-5 days elimination half-life Phenobarbital	**Indicate the hypnotic benzodiazepine, which has the shortest elimination half-life** Triazolam
Which hypnotic drugs is more likely to cause cumulative and residual effects? Phenobarbital	**Which hypnotic drugs increases the activity of hepatic drug-metabolizing enzyme systems?** Phenobarbital

Hepatic microsomal drug-metabolizing enzyme induction leads to Barbiturate tolerance	True or False. Hypnotic benzodiazepines are more powerful enzyme inducers than barbiturates. FALSE
Indicate the hypnotic drug, which does not change hepatic drug-metabolizing enzyme activity? - Flurazepam- Zaleplon- Triazolam	Barbiturates increase the rate of metabolism of - Anticoagulants- Digitalis compounds- Glucocorticoids
Which agents inhibits hepatic metabolism of hypnotics? Cimetidin	Which factors can influence the biodisposition of hypnotic agents? - Alterations in the hepatic function resulting from a disease- Old age- Drug-induced increases or decreases in microsomal enzyme activities
Which hypnotics is preferred for elderly patients? Temazepam	Which hypnotics is preferred in patients with limited hepatic function? Zolpidem
Indicate the mechanism of barbiturate action (at hypnotic doses) Increasing the duration of the GABA-gated Cl-channel openings	Imidazopyridines are Selective agonists of the BZ1 (omega1) subtype of BZ receptors

Which hypnotic agents is a positive allosteric modulator of GABA-A receptor function? - Zaleplon- Flurazepam- Zolpidem	**Indicate a hypnotic drug - a selective agonist at the BZ1 receptor subtype** Zolpidem
Which hypnotic agents is able to interact with both BZ1 and BZ2 receptor subtypes? Flurazepam	**Indicate the competitive antagonist of BZ receptors** Flumazenil
Flumazenil blocks the actions of Zolpidem	**Indicate the agent, which interferes with GABA binding** Bicuculline
Which agents blocks the chloride channel directly? Picrotoxin	**Which agents is preferred in the treatment of insomnia?** Hypnotic benzodiazepines
Barbiturates are being replaced by hypnotic benzodiazepines because of - Low therapeutic index- Suppression in REM sleep- High potential of physical dependence and abuse	**Which benzodiazepines is used mainly for hypnosis?** Flurazepam

Indicate the main claim for an ideal hypnotic agent - Rapid onset and sufficient duration of action - Minor effects on sleep patterns - Minimal "hangover" effects	**Which stage of sleep is responsible for the incidence of dreams?** REM sleep
During slow wave sleep (stage 3 and 4 NREM sleep) Somnambulism and nightmares occur	**All of the hypnotic drugs induce** Decrease the duration of REM sleep
Which hypnotic drugs causes least suppression of REM sleep? Flurazepam	**Although the benzodiazepines continue to be the agents of choice for insomnia, they have** - The possibility of psychological and physiological dependence - Synergistic depression of CNS with other drugs (especially alcohol) - Residual drowsiness and daytime sedation
Hypnotic benzodiazepines can cause A dose-dependent decrease in both REM and slow wave sleep	**Which hypnotic benzodiazepines is more likely to cause rebound insomnia?** Triazolam
Which hypnotic benzodiazepines is more likely to cause "hangover" effects such as drowsiness, dysphoria, and mental or motor depression the following day? Flurazepam	**Indicate the hypnotic drug, which binds selectively to the BZ1 receptor subtype, facilitating GABAergic inhibition** Zolpidem

Which agent exerts hypnotic activity with minimal muscle relaxing and anticonvulsant effects? Zaleplon	True or False. Zolpidem and zaleplon have effectiveness similar to that of hypnotic benzodiazepines in the management of sleep disorders. TRUE
Which hypnotic drugs is used intravenously as anesthesia? Thiopental	Indicate the usual cause of death due to overdose of hypnotics Depression of the medullar respiratory center
Toxic doses of hypnotics may cause a circulatory collapse as a result of Action on the medullar vasomotor center	The mechanism of action of antiseizure drugs is - Enhancement of GABAergic (inhibitory) transmission- Diminution of excitatory (usually glutamatergic) transmission- Modification of ionic conductance
Which antiseizure drugs produces enhancement of GABA-mediated inhibition? Phenobarbital	Indicate an antiseizure drug, which has an impotent effect on the T-type calcium channels in thalamic neurons? Ethosuximide
Which antiseizure drugs produces a voltage-dependent inactivation of sodium channels? - Lamotrigine- Carbamazepin- Phenytoin	Indicate an antiseizure drug, inhibiting central effects of excitatory amino acids Lamotrigine

The drug for partial and generalized tonic-clonic seizures is - Carbamazepine- Valproate- Phenytoin	Indicate an anti-absence drug Valproate
The drug against myoclonic seizures is Clonazepam	The most effective drug for stopping generalized tonic-clonic status epilepticus in adults is Diazepam
Phenytoin It blocks sodium channels	Phenytoin is used in the treatment of Grand mal epilepsy
Dose-related adverse effect caused by phenytoin is Gingival hyperplasia	Granulocytopenia, gastrointestinal irritation, gingival hyperplasia, and facial hirsutism are possible adverse effects of Phenytoin
The antiseizure drug, which induces hepatic microsomal enzymes, is Phenytoin	The drug of choice for partial seizures is Carbamazepin

The mechanism of action of carbamazepine appears to be similar to that of Phenytoin	Which antiseizure drugs is also effective in treating trigeminal neuralgia? Carbamazepine
The most common dose-related adverse effects of carbamazepine are Diplopia, ataxia, and nausea	Indicate the drug of choice for status epilepticus in infants and children Phenobarbital sodium
Barbiturates are used in the emergency treatment of status epilepticus in infants and children because of They significantly decrease of oxygen utilization by the brain, protecting cerebral edema and ischemia	Which antiseizure drugs binds to an allosteric regulatory site on the GABA-BZ receptor, increases the duration of the Cl-channels openings Phenobarbital
Adverse effect caused by phenobarbital is - Physical and phychological dependence- Exacerbated petit mal epilepsy- Sedation	Which antiseizure drugs is a prodrug, metabolized to phenobarbital? Primidone
Indicate the antiseizure drug, which is a phenyltriazine derivative Lamotrigine	Lamotrigine can be used in the treatment of - Partial seizures- Absence- Myoclonic seizures

The mechanism of vigabatrin's action is Inhibition of GABA aminotransferase	Indicate an irreversible inhibitor of GABA aminotransferase (GABA-T) Vigabatrin
Tiagabine Blocks neuronal and glial reuptake of GABA from synapses	The mechanism of both topiramate and felbamate action is - Reduction of excitatory glutamatergic neurotransmission - Inhibition of voltage sensitive Na+ channels - Potentiation of GABAergic neuronal transmission
The drug of choice in the treatment of petit mal (absence seizures) is Ethosuximide	The dose-related adverse effect of ethosuximide is - Gastrointestinal reactions, such as anorexia, pain, nausea and vomiting - Exacerbated grand mal epilepsy - Transient lethargy or fatigue
Valproate is very effective against - Absence seizures - Myoclonic seizures - Generalized tonic-clonic seizures	The drug of choice in the treatment of myoclonic seizures is Valproate
The reason for preferring ethosuximide to valproate for uncomplicated absence seizures is Valproate's idiosyncratic hepatotoxicity	Indicate the antiseizure drug, which is a sulfonamide derivative, blocking Na+ channels and having additional ability to inhibit T-type Ca2+ channels Zonisamide

Question	Answer
Indicate the antiseizure drug – a benzodiazepine receptor agonist	Lorazepam
Which antiseizure drugs acts directly on the GABA receptor-chloride channel complex?	Diazepam
Benzodiazepine's uselfulness is limited by	Tolerance
A long-acting drug against both absence and myoclonic seizures is	Clonazepam
Which antiseizure drugs may produce teratogenicity?	- Phenytoin - Valproate - Topiramate
The most dangerous effect of antiseizure drugs after large overdoses is	Respiratory depression
Which neurons are involved in parkinsonism?	- Cholinergic neurons - GABAergic neurons - Dopaminergic neurons
The pathophysiologic basis for antiparkinsonism therapy is	A selective loss of dopaminergic neurons
Which neurotransmitters is involved in Parkinson's disease?	- Acetylcholine - Glutamate - Dopamine
True or False. The concentration of dopamine in the basal ganglia of the brain is reduced in parkinsonism.	TRUE

Indicate the drug that induces parkinsonian syndromes Chlorpromazine	Which drugs is used in the treatment of Parkinsonian disorders Selegiline
Select the agent, which is preferred in the treatment of the drug-induced form of parkinsonism Benztropine	Which agents is the precursor of dopamine? Levodopa
The main reason for giving levodopa, the precursor of dopamine, instead of dopamine is Dopamine does not cross the blood-brain barrier	Indicate a peripheral dopa decarboxylase inhibitor Carbidopa
The mechanism of carbidopa's action is Inhibition of dopa decarboxilase	True or False. Carbidopa is unable to penetrate the blood-brain barrier, it acts to reduce the peripheral conversion of levodopa to dopamine. TRUE
Which preparations combines carbidopa and levodopa in a fixed proportion? Sinemet	Gastrointestinal irritation, cardiovascular effects, including tachycardia, arrhythmias, and orthostatic hypotension, mental disturbances, and withdrawal are possible adverse effects of Levodopa

Question	Answer
Which agents is the most helpful in counteracting the behavioral complications of levodopa?	Clozapine
Which vitamins reduces the beneficial effects of levodopa by enhancing its extracerebral metabolism?	Pyridoxine
Which drugs antagonizes the effects of levodopa because it leads to a junctional blockade of dopamine action?	- Reserpine - Haloperidol - Chlorpromazine
Levodopa should not be given to patients taking	Monoamine oxydase A inhibitors
Indicate D2 receptor agonist with antiparkinsonian activity	Bromocriptine
Which antiparkinsonian drugs has also been used to treat hyperprolactinemia?	Bromocriptine
Indicate a selective inhibitor of monoamine oxidase B	Selegiline
True or False. MAO-A metabolizes norepinephrine and serotonin, MAO-B metabolizes dopamine	TRUE
True or False. Treatment with selegilin postpones the need for levodopa for 3-9 months and may retard the progression of Parkinson's disease.	TRUE
The main reason for avoiding the combined administration of levodopa and an inhibitor of both forms of monoamine oxidase is	Hypertensive emergency

Indicate selective catechol-O-methyltransferase inhibitor, which prolongs the action of levodopa by diminishing its peripheral metabolism Tolcapone	Which antiparkinsonian drugs is an antiviral agent used in the prophylaxis of influenza A2? Amantadine
The mechanism of amantadine action is Stimulating the glutamatergic neurotransmission	Which antiparkinsonism drugs is an anticholinergic agent? Trihexyphenidyl
Mental confusion and hallucinations, peripheral atropine like toxicity (e.g. Cycloplegia, tachycardia, urinary retention, and constipation) are possible adverse effects of Benztropine	Indicate the antiparkinsonism drug which should be avoided in patients with glaucoma Trihexyphenidyl
Alcohol may cause - CNS depression- Vasodilatation- Hypoglycemia	Alcohol Increases body heat loss
True or False. It is undesirable to take alcohol before going outdoors when it extremely cold, but it may be harmless to take some after coming into a warm place from the cold. TRUE	The most common medical complication of alcohol abuse is - Liver failure including liver cirrhosis- Tolerance and physical dependence- Generalized symmetric peripheral nerve injury, ataxia and dementia

Effect of moderate consumption of alcohol on plasma lipoproteins is Raising serum levels of high-density lipoproteins	**Which metabolic alterations may be associated with chronic alcohol abuse?** Severe loss of potassium and magnesium
Alcohol potentiates - SNS depressants - Vasodilatators - Hypoglycemic agents	**Which drugs is most commonly used for causing a noxious reaction to alcohol by blocking its metabolism?** Disulfiram
Which agents is an inhibitor of aldehyde dehydrogenase? Disulfiram	**Indicate the drug, which alters brain responses to alcohol** Naltrexone
Which agents is an opioid antagonist? Naltrexone	**Alcohol causes an acute increase in the local concentrations of** - Dopamine - Opioid - Serotonine
Management of alcohol withdrawal syndrome contains - Restoration of potassium, magnesium and phosphate balance - Thiamine therapy - Substituting a long-acting sedative-hypnotic drug for alcohol	**Indicate the drug, which decreases the craving for alcohol or blunts pleasurable "high" that comes with renewed drinking** Naltrexone

The symptoms resulting from the combination of disulfiram and alcohol are Nausea, vomiting	The combination of disulfiram and ethanol leads to accumulation of Acetaldehyde
True or False. The combination of naltrexone and disulfiram should be avoided since both drugs are potential hepatotoxins. TRUE	Indicate the "specific" modality of treatment for severe methanol poisoning - Dialysis to enhance removal of methanol- Alkalinization to counteract metabolic acidosis- Suppression of metabolism by alcohol dehydrogenase to toxic products
Which agents may be used as an antidote for ethylene glycol and methanol poisoning? Fomepizol	The principal mechanism of fomepizol action is associated with inhibition of Alcohol dehydrogenase
Narcotics analgesics should Relieve severe pain	Second-order pain is Dull, burning pain
Chemical mediators in the nociceptive pathway are - Kinins- Prostaglandins- Substance P	Chemical mediators in the nociceptive pathway are not Enkephalins

Indicate the chemical mediator in the antinociceptive descending pathways - BETA-endorphin- Met- and leu-enkephalin- Dynorphin	**Which mediators is found mainly in long descending pathways from the midbrain to the dorsal horn?** Enkephalin
Select the brain and spinal cord regions, which are involved in the transmission of pain? - The limbic system, including the amygdaloidal nucleus and the hypothalamus- The ventral and medial parts of the thalamus- The substantia gelatinosa	**Mu (μ) receptors are associated with** Analgesia, euphoria, respiratory depression, physical dependence
Which opioid receptor types is responsible for euphoria and respiratory depression? Mu (μ) receptors	**Indicate the opioid receptor type, which is responsible for dysphoria and vasomotor stimulation** Kappa-receptors
Kappa and delta agonists Close a voltage-gated Ca2+ channels on presynaptic nerve terminals	**Which supraspinal structures is implicated in pain-modulating descending pathways?** The midbrain periaqueductal gray
Indicate the neurons, which are located in the locus ceruleus or the lateral tegmental area of the reticular formation Nonadrenergic	**Which analgesics is a phenanthrene derivative?** Morphine

Q	A
Tick narcotic analgesic, which is a phenylpiperidine derivative	Fentanyl
Which opioid analgesics is a strong mu receptor agonist?	Morphine
Indicate the narcotic analgesic, which is a natural agonist	Morphine
Select the narcotic analgesic, which is an antagonist or partial mu receptor agonist	Pentazocine
Which agents is a full antagonist of opioid receptors?	Naloxone
The principal central nervous system effect of the opioid analgesics with affinity for a mu receptor is	- Analgesia - Respiratory depression - Euphoria
Which opioid analgesics can produce dysphoria, anxiety and hallucinations?	Pentazocine
Which opioid analgesics is used in combination with droperidol in neuroleptanalgesia?	Fentanyl
Fentanyl can produce significant respiratory depression by	- Suppression of the cough reflex leading to airway obstruction - Development of truncal rigidity
Most strong mu receptor agonists cause	Cerebral vasodilatation, causing an increase in intracranial pressure

Which opioid analgesics can produce an increase in the pulmonary arterial pressure and myocardial work? Pentazocine	**Morphine causes** - Constipation- Urinary retention- Bronchiolar constriction
Morphine do not causes Dilatation of the biliary duct	**Therapeutic doses of the opioid analgesics** Decrease body temperature
Which opioid analgesics is used in obstetric labor? Meperidine	**Indicate the opioid analgesic, which is used for relieving the acute, severe pain of renal colic** Meperidine
Which opioid analgesics is used in the treatment of acute pulmonary edema? Morphine	**The relief produced by intravenous morphine in dyspnea from pulmonary edema is associated with reduced** - Perception of shortness of breath- Patient anxiety- Cardiac preload (reduced venous tone) and afterload (decreased peripheral resistance)
Rhinorrhea, lacrimation, chills, gooseflesh, hyperventilation, hyperthermia, mydriasis, muscular aches, vomiting, diarrhea, anxiety, and hostility are effects of Abstinence syndrome	**The diagnostic triad of opioid overdosage is** Coma, depressed respiration and miosis

Which opioid agents is used in the treatment of acute opioid overdose? Naloxone	**Indicate the pure opioid antagonist, which has a half-life of 10 hours** Naltrexone
In contrast to morphine, methadone - Causes tolerance and physical dependence more slowly- Is more effective orally- Withdrawal is less severe, although more prolonged	**Which opioid analgesics is a partial mu receptor agonist?** Buprenorphine
Indicate a partial mu receptor agonist, which has 20-60 times analgesic potency of morphine, and a longer duration of action Buprenorphine	**Which opioid analgesics is a strong kappa receptor agonist and a mu receptor antagonist?** Nalbuphine
Which drugs has weak mu agonist effects and inhibitory action on norepinephrine and serotonin reuptake in the CNS? Tramadol	**Non-narcotic analgesics are mainly effective against pain associated with** Inflammation or tissue damage
Non-narcotic agents cause Antipyretic effect	**Non-narcotic analgesics are** - Paracetamol- Acetylsalicylic acid- Ketorolac

Non-narcotic analgesics are not Butorphanol	**Select the non-narcotic drug, which is a paraaminophenol derivative** Paracetamol
Which of the following non-narcotic agents is salicylic acid derivative? Aspirin	**Tick pirazolone derivative** Analgin
Which non-narcotic agents inhibits mainly cyclooxygenase (COX) in CNS? Paracetamol	**Most of non-narcotic analgetics have** - Anti-inflammatory effect- Analgesic effect- Antipyretic effect
Indicate the non-narcotic analgesic, which lacks an anti-inflammatory effect Paracetamol	**True or False about aspirin. It inhibits mainly peripheral COX** TRUE
True or False about aspirin. It does not have an anti-inflammatory effect FALSE	**True or False about aspirin. It inhibits platelet aggregation.** TRUE

True or False about aspirin. It stimulates respiration by a direct action on the respiratory center TRUE	For which conditions could aspirin be used prophylactically? Thromboembolism
All of the following are undesirable effects of aspirin - Gastritis with focal erosions- Bleeding due to a decrease of platelet aggregation- Reversible renal insufficiency	Is not a Undesirable effects of aspirin Tolerance and physical addiction
Characteristic findinds of salicylism include - Headache, mental confusion and drowsiness- Tinnitus and difficulty in hearing- Hyperthermia, sweating, thirst, hyperventilation, vomiting and diarrhea	Analgin usefulness is limited by Agranulocytosis
Methemoglobinemia is possible adverse effect of Paracetamol	True or False for ketorolac. It inhibits COX TRUE
True or False for ketorolac. It is as effective as morphine for a short-term relief from moderate to severe pain TRUE	True or False for ketorolac. It has a high potential for physical dependence and abuse FALSE

True or False for ketorolac. It does not produce respiratory depression TRUE	Indicate the nonopioid agent of central effect with analgesic activity Clopheline
Select the antiseizure drug with an analgesic component of effect Carbamazepine	Which nonopioid agents is an antidepressant with analgesic activity? Amitriptyline
Tick mixed (opioid/non-opioid) agent Tramadol	Neuroleptics are used to treat Psychosis
Most antipsychotic drugs Strongly block postsynaptic d2receptor	Which dopaminergic systems is most closely related to behavior? The mesolimbic and mesofrontal systems
Hyperprolactinemia is caused by blockade of dopamine in The pituitary	Parkinsonian symptoms and tarditive dyskinesia are caused by blockade dopamine in The nigrostriatal system

Extrapyramidal reactions can be treated by	True or False. D1 postsynaptic receptors are located in striatum
Benztropine mesylate	TRUE

True or False. D2 pre- and postsynaptic receptors are located in striatum and limbic areas	True or False. D4 postsynaptic receptors are located in frontal cortex, mesolimbic system
TRUE	TRUE

Which antipsychotic drugs is typical?	Indicate the atypical antipsychotic drug
Haloperidol	Clozapine

Atypical antipsychotic agents (such as clozapine) differ from typical ones	Tardive dyskinesia is the result of
- In reduced risks of extrapyramidal system dysfunction and tardive dyscinesia- In having low affinity for D1 and D2 dopamine receptors- In having high affinity for D4 dopamine receptors	Hyperactive dopaminergic state in the presence of dopamine blockers

Which antipsychotic drugs has high affinity for D4 and 5-HT2 receptors?	Indicate the antipsychotic drug, which is a phenothiazine aliphatic derivative
Clozapine	Chlorpromazine

Indicate the antipsychotic drug, which is a butyrophenone derivative Droperidol	**Indicate the antipsychotic drug, which is a thioxanthene derivative** Thiothixene
Indicate the antipsychotic agent – a dibenzodiazepine derivative Clozapine	**The strong antiemetic effect of the phenothiazine derivatives is due to dopamine receptor blockade** - In the chemoreceptor trigger zone of the medulla- Of the receptors in the stomach- The medullar vomiting centre
Phenothiazine derivatives are able to Alter temperature-regulating mechanisms producing hypothermia	**Most phenothiazine derivatives have** - Antihistaminic activity- Anticholinergic activity- Antidopaminergic activity
Indicate the antipsychotic drug having significant peripheral alpha-adrenergic blocking activity Chlorpromazine	**Indicate the antipsychotic drug having a muscarinic-cholinergic blocking activity** Chlorpromazine
Indicate the antipsychotic drug having H1-antihistaminic activity - Clozapine- Chlorpromazine- Olanzapine	**Parkinson's syndrome, acute dystonic reactions, tardive dyskinesia, antimuscarinic actions, orthostatic hypotension, galactorrhea are possible adverse effects of** Chlorpromazine

Orthostatic hypotension can occur as a result of - The central action of phenothiazines - Inhibition of norepinephrine uptake mechanisms - Alpha adrenoreceptor blockade	Adverse peripheral effects, such as loss of accommodation, dry mouth, tachycardia, urinary retention, constipation are related to Muscarinic cholinoreceptor blockade
Which phenothiazine derivatives is a potent local anesthetic? Chlorpromazine	Which phenothiazine derivatives may produce cardiac toxicity, including ventricular arrhythmias, cardiac conduction block, and sudden death? Thioridazine
Which antipsychotic agents is preferable in patients with coronary and cerebrovascular disease? Haloperidol	Which antipsychotic agents is used in combination with an opioid drug fentanyl in neuroleptanalgesia? Droperidol
The mechanism of haloperidol antipsychotic action is - Blocking D2 receptors - Central alpha-adrenergic blocking - Inhibition of norepinephrine uptake mechanisms	True or False about clozapine. Has potent anticholinergic activity TRUE
True or False about clozapine. Has high affinity for D1 and D2 dopamine receptors FALSE	True or False about clozapine. Produces significant extrapyramidal toxicity FALSE

True or False about clozapine. Is related to typical antipsychotic agents FALSE	Which antipsychotic drugs has the high risk of potentially fatal agranulocytosis and risk of seizures at high doses? Clozapine
Which antipsychotic drugs has high affinity for D2 and 5-HT2 receptors? Risperidone	Lithium carbonate is useful in the treatment of Bipolar disorder
The drug of choice for manic-depressive psychosis is Lithium carbonate	The lithium mode of action is - Effect on electrolytes and ion transport- Effect on neurotransmitters- Effect on second messengers
True or False about lithium. Stimulate dopamine and beta-adrenergic receptors FALSE	True or False about lithium. Decrease catecholamine-related activity TRUE
True or False about lithium. Stimulate the development of dopamine receptor supersensitivity FALSE	True or False about lithium. Decrease cholinergic activity FALSE

Question	Answer
Which adverse effects is associated with lithium treatment?	- Cardiovascular anomalies in the newborn - Thyroid enlargement - Nephrogenic diabetes insipidus
The principal mechanism of action of antidepressant agents is	Blocking epinephrine or serotonin reuptake pumps
Which agents is related to tricyclic antidepressants?	Amitriptyline
Indicate the second-generation heterocyclic drug	Maprotiline
Which agents is related to the third-generation heterocyclic antidepressants?	Nefazodone
Which antidepressants is a selective serotonin reuptake inhibitor?	Fluoxetine
Which antidepressant agents is a selective inhibitor of norepinephrine reuptake?	Maprotiline
Indicate the antidepressant, which blocks the reuptake pumps for serotonin and norepinephrine	Amitriptyline
Which antidepressants is an unselective MAO blocker and produces extremely long-lasting inhibition of the enzyme?	Tranylcypramine
Indicate the irreversible MAO inhibitor, which is a hydrazide derivative	Phenelzine

Which MAO inhibitors has amphetamine-like activity and is related to nonhydrazide derivatives Tranylcypramine	**Which antidepressants is a selective short-acting MAO-A inhibitor?** Moclobemide
Monoamine Oxydase A Is responsible for norepinephrine, serotonin, and tyramine metabolism	**Which synapses are involved in depression?** Serotoninergic synapses
Block of which type of Monoamine Oxydase might be more selective for depression? MAO-A	**The principal mechanism of MAO inhibitor action is** Blocking a major degradative pathway for the amine neurotransmitters, which permits more amines to accumulate in presynaptic stores
The irreversible MAO inhibitors have a very high risk of developing Hypertensive reactions to tyramine ingested in food	**The most dangerous pharmacodynamic interaction is between MAO inhibitors and** - Selective serotonin reuptake inhibitors- Tricyclics- Sympathomimetics
Serotonin syndrome is a result of - Increased stores of monoamine- Significant accumulation of amine neurotransmitters in the synapses	**The therapeutic response to antidepressant drugs is usually over a period of** 2-3 weeks

Which antidepressants may have latency period as short as 48 hours?	Which features do MAO inhibitors and tricyclic antidepressants have in common?
Tranylcypromine	Increase levels of biogenic amines
Tricyclic antidepressants are	Which autonomic nervous system effects is common for tricyclic antidepressants?
Mixed norepinephrine and serotonin reuptake inhibitors	- Antimuscarinic action - Antihistaminic action - Alfa adrenoreceptor-blocking action
Indicate an effective antidepressant with minimal autonomic toxicity	Fluoxetine has fewer adverse effects because of
Fluoxetine	Minimal binding to cholinergic, histaminic, and alfa-adrenergic receptors
Which tricyclic and heterocyclic antidepressants has the greatest sedation?	Which tricyclic and heterocyclic agents has the least sedation?
- Doxepin - Amitriptyline - Trazodone	Protriptyline
Indicate a tricyclic or a heterocyclic antidepressant having greatest antimuscarinic effects	Indicate a tricyclic or a heterocyclic antidepressant having least antimuscarinic effects
Amitriptyline	- Trazodone - Buprorion - Mirtazapine

Which antidepressants has significant alfa2-adrenoreceptor antagonism? Mirtazapine	**Indicate the main claim for an ideal antidepressant agent** - A faster onset of action- Fewer adverse sedative and autonomic effects- Fewer toxicity when overdoses are taken
Which drugs is least likely to be prescribed to patients with prostatic hypertrophy, glaucoma, coronary and cerebrovascular disease? Amitriptyline	**Indicate the antidepressant agent, which is a phenyltolylpropylamine derivative** Fluoxetine
The mechanism of fluoxetine action includes - Selective inhibition of serotonine uptake in the CNS- Little effect on central norepinephrine or dopamine function- Minimal binding to cholinergic, histaminic, and alfa-adrenergic receptors	**Which antidepressants is used for treatment of eating disorders, especially buliemia?** Fluoxetine
True or False. Sertaline and paroxetine are similar to fluoxetine in the mechanism of action and therapeutic use, sertaline is less likely to interact adversely with other drugs. TRUE	**A highly selective serotonin reuptake inhibitor is** - Sertaline- Paroxetine- Fluoxetine
Anxiolytics are used to treat Neurosis	**Anxiolytic agents should** Reduce anxiety and exert a calming effect

Anxiolytics are also useful for - Treatment of epilepsy and seizures - Insomnia - Muscle relaxation in specific neuromuscular disorders	**Indicate the agents of choice in the treatment of most anxiety states** Benzodiazepines
The choice of benzodiazepines for anxiety is based on - A relatively high therapeutic index - Availability of flumazenil for treatment of overdose - A low risk of physiologic dependence	**Which anxiolitics is a benzodiazepine derivative** Clordiazepoxide
Indicate the benzodiazepine, which has the shortest elimination half-life Triazolam	**Which benzodiazepines has the shortest duration of action?** Triazolam
Which benzodiazepines is less likely to cause cumulative and residual effects with multiple doses? Lorazepam	**Anxiolytic dosage reduction is recommended** - In patients taking cimetidine - In patients with hepatic dysfunction - In elderly patients
Which benzodiazepines is preferred for elderly patients? Triazolam	**Which anxiolytics is preferred in patient with limited hepatic function?** Buspirone

Indicate the mechanism of hypnotic benzodiazepine action Increasing the frequency of Cl- channel opening events	**Which anxiolytics is a partial agonist of brain 5-HT1A receptors?** Buspirone
Indicate the competitive antagonist of BZ receptors Flumazenil	**Indicate the agent, which interferes with GABA binding** Bicuculline
Antianxiety agents have - Sedative and hypnotic activity- Muscle relaxing and anticonvulsant effects- Amnesic properties	**Which disadvantages does not limit using benzodiazepines as antianxiety agents?** A high risk of drug interactions based on liver enzyme induction
Indicate the anxiolitic agent, which relieves anxiety without causing marked sedative effects Buspirone	**Which anxiolytics has minimal abuse liability?** Buspirone
In contrast to benzodiazepines, buspirone Causes less psychomotor impairment and does not affect driving skills	**Which sedative-hypnotic drugs does not potentiate the CNS depressant effects of ethanol, phenothiazines, or tricyclic antidepressants?** Buspirone

Limitation of buspirone is An extremely slow onset of action	**Which drugs may be used as antianxiety agents?** - BETA-blocking drugs- Clonidine - a partial agonist of alfa2 receptors- Tricyclic antidepressants
Which benzodiazepines is more likely to cause "hangover" effects such as drowsiness, dysphoria, and mental or motor depression the following day? Clorazepat	**Additive CNS depression can be predicted if benzodiazepines are used with** - Ethanol- Morphine- Clorpromazine
Which dosage of benzodiazepines for 60-90 days may produce severe withdrawal symptoms? 50-60 mg/d	**Restlessness, anxiety, orthostatic hypotension, generalized seizures, severe tremor, vivid hallucination, and psychosis are possible symptoms of** Withdrawal
Flumazenil given intravenously Acts rapidly but has a short half-life	**Agents, stimulating CNS are** - Fluoxetine- Nootropil- Sydnocarb
Which CNS stimulants are the agents of selective effect? Psychostimulants	**Indicate CNC stimulating drugs, which are the agents of general action** Analeptics

Which agents belongs to psychostimulants? Meridil	**Indicate the nootropic agent** Piracetam
Which agents is a respiratory analeptic? Bemegride	**Indicate the CNC stimulating drug, which belongs to adaptogens** Eleuterococci extract
Actoprotectors are Stimulators, improving physical efficiency	**Adaptogens cause** Increased resistance towards stress situations and adaptation to extreme conditions
Indicate the CNS stimulants, which mitigate conditions of weakness or lack of tone within the entire organism or in particular organs? General tonics	**Which agents is a general tone-increasing drug of plant origin?** Eleuterococci's extract
Indicate a general tone-increasing drug, which is an agent of animal origin? Pantocrin	**Amphetamine** - Is a powerful stimulant of the CNS- Stimulates the medullar respiratory center and has an analeptic action- Increases motor and speech activity, mood, decreases a sense of fatigue

The mechanism of amphetamine action is related to - Direct catecholamiergic agonist action- Inhibition of monoamine oxydase- Increasing a release of catecholaminergic neurotransmitters	**Indicate the CNS stimulant, which is a piperidine derivative** Meridil
Which CNS psychostimulants is a sydnonymine derivative? Sydnocarb	**Sydnocarb causes** Decreased sense of fatigue, it facilitates the professional work and fights somnolence
Indicate the psychostimulant, which is a methylxantine derivative Caffeine	**Which of the following psychostimulants acts centrally mainly by blocking adenosine receptors?** Caffeine
Principal properties of caffeine do not include Adaptogenic (rise non-specific resistance towards stresses and adapt to extraordinary challenges)	**Caffeine can produce** - Coronary vasodialation- Relaxation of bronchial and biliary tract smooth muscles- Reinforcement of the contractions and increase of the striaated muscle work
Caffeine can not produce Vasodialation of cerebral vessels	**Caffeine does not cause** Inhibition of gastric secretion

Caffeine cause - Hyperglycemia - Moderate diuretic action - Increase in free fatty acids	**Therapeutic uses of caffeine include** - Cardiovascular collapse and respiratory insufficiency - Migraine - Somnolence
Therapeutic uses of caffeine do not include Gastric ulceration	**Adverse effects of caffeine include** - Arrhythmias - Insomnia - Psychomotor excitation
Adverse effects of caffeine do not include Hypotension	**Principal properties of cordiamine include** - Cardiac analeptic - Respiratory analeptic - Coronarodilatator
Principal properties of cordiamine do not include Significant abuse potential	**Characteristics of cordiamine do not include** It decreases the aortic and coronary flow
Cordiamine is useful in the treatment of - Hypotension - Coronary insufficiency - Respiratory insufficiency	**Respiratory and cardiac analeptics are the agents** - Cordiamine - Caffeine - Camphor

Respiratory and cardiac analeptics are not the agents Bemegride	Bemegride Stimulates the medullar respiratory center (central effect)
Which CNS stimulants belongs to nootropics? Piracetam	Characteristics of nootropics include - Selective influence on the brain- Improvement the ability to communicate with peers- Increase in energetic exchange of the brain cells
Characteristics of nootropics do not include Decline in the highest integrative brain functions	True or False about Nootropics. They improve the highest integrative brain functions (memory, learning, understanding, thinking and the capacity for concentration) TRUE
True or False about Nootropics. They stimulate the bulbar respiratory center FALSE	True or False about Nootropics. They stimulate existing neuronal synapses to optimum performance (adaptive capacity) TRUE
Features of piracetam include - It is a GABA derivative- It does not influence the neuro-vegetative function- Improvement begins in the 3'rd week	Features of piracetam do not include It has a high potential of toxicity

Piracetam can produce - Anticonvulsant - Psychometabolic - Antihypoxic	**Piracetam can not produce** Antipsychotic
Piracetam is widely used for the treatment of - Senile dementia - Asthenia - Chronic alcoholism	**Which CNS stimulants is used for the cerebral stroke treatment?** Piracetam
Psychologic dependence is Compulsive drug-seeking behavior	**Tolerance is associated with** - An ability to compensate for the drug effect - Increased disposition of the drug after chronic use - Compensatory changes in receptors, effector enzymes, or membrane actions of the drug
Addiction is associated with the existence of - Psychological dependence - Physiological dependence - Tolerance	**Substances causing narco- and glue sniffings are** - Stimulants - Psychedelics - Sedative drugs
Substances causing narco- and glue sniffings are not Antipsychotic drugs	**Which abused drugs do not belong to sedative agents?** Cannabinoids

Psychedelics are	Psychedelics are not
- LSD- Marijuana- Volatile substances (glues, solvents, volatile nitrites and nitrous oxide)	Cocaine
In contrast to morphine, heroin is	True or False. Symptoms of opioid withdrawal begin 8-10 hours after the last dose.
More addictive and fast-acting	TRUE
The acute course of opioid withdrawal may last	Indicate the sedative-hypnotic agent, which has the highest abuse potential
7-10 days	Phenobarbital
Characteristics of barbiturate intoxication (2-3 dose) do not include	Barbiturate abstinent syndrome is shown by
Perceptual distortion of surroundings, disorders of thinking, behavior	- Crisis by 3 day of abstention- Anxiety, mydriasis, myasthenia, muscular convulsions, vomiting, diarrhea- Psychosis as delirium (color visual and auditory hallucinations)
Which tranquilizers belongs to strong euphorizing agents?	Tranquilizers intoxication (5-10 tablets) features include:
Diazepam	Euphoria, burst of energy, increase in motor activity, wave warmth all over the body

Which abused drugs is related to stimulants?	Cocaine exerts its central action by
- Cocaine - Amphetamine - Caffeine	Inhibiting dopamine and norepinephrine reuptake

"Crack" is a derivative of	Which stimulants is related to psychedelics?
Cocaine	"ecstasy" (methylenedioxymethamphetamine)

Cocaine may cause	Characteristics of cocaine abstinent syndrome do not include
- Powerful vasoconstrictive reactions resulting in myocardial infarctions - The multiple brain perfusion defects - Spontaneous abortion during pregnancy	Psychosis as color visual and auditory hallucinations (for 3 day)

Overdoses of cocaine are usually rapidly fatal from	Which agents is related to hallucinogens?
- Respiratory depression - Arrhythmias - Seizures	LSD

LSD produces	LSD decreases in brain
- Mood swings - Impaired memory, difficulty in thinking, poor judgment - Perceptual distortion	5-HT2 receptor densities

Which agents is related to cannabis? Hashish	**The early stage of cannabis intoxication is characterized by** - Euphoria, uncontrolled laugher- Alteration of time sense, depersonalization- Sharpened vision
Which physiologic signs is a characteristic of cannabis intoxication? Reddening of the conjunctiva	**Industrial solvent inhalation causes** - Quick intoxication, lasting only 5-15 minutes- Euphoria, relaxed "drunk" feeling- Disorientation, slow passage of time and possible hallucinations
Indicate the drugs of choice for reversing the withdrawal syndrome - Benzodiazepines- Neuroleptics- Antidepressants	**The state of "general anesthesia" usually includes** - Analgesia- Loss of consciousness, inhibition of sensory and autonomic reflexes- Amnesia
Inhaled anesthetics and intravenous agents having general anesthetic properties Directly activate GABAA receptors	**Indicate the anesthetic, which is an inhibitor of NMDA glutamate receptors:** Ketamine
An ideal anesthetic drug would - Induces anesthesia smoothly and rapidly and secure rapid recovery- Posses a wide margin of safety- Be devoid of adverse effects	**Which general anesthetics belongs to inhalants?** Desfluran

Indicate the anesthetic, which is used intravenously Propofol	**Which inhalants is a gas anesthetic?** Nitrous oxide
Sevoflurane has largely replaced halothane and isoflurane as an inhalation anesthetic of choice because - Induction of anesthesia is achieved more rapidly and smoothly- Recovery is more rapid- It has low post- anesthetic organ toxicity	**The limitation of sevoflurane is** Chemically unstable
Which inhalants lacks sufficient potency to produce surgical anesthesia by itself and therefore is commonly used with another inhaled or intravenous anesthetic? Nitrous oxide	**Which inhaled anesthetics has rapid onset and recovery?** - Nitrous oxide- Desflurane- Sevoflurane
Indicate the inhaled anesthetic, which reduces arterial pressure and heart rate Halothane	**Which inhaled anesthetics causes centrally mediated sympathetic activation leading to a rise in blood pressure and heart rate?** Desflurane
Indicated the inhaled anesthetic, which decreases the ventilatory response to hypoxia Nitrous oxide	**Which inhaled anesthetics is an induction agent of choice in patient with airway problems?** Halothane

Indicate the inhaled anesthetic, which causes the airway irritation Desflurane	Which inhaled anesthetics increases cerebral blood flow least of all? Nitrous oxide
Indicate the inhaled anesthetic, which should be avoided in patients with a history of seizure disorders Enflurane	Which inhaled anesthetics can produce hepatic necrosis? Halothane
Indicated the inhaled anesthetic, which may cause nephrotoxicity Soveflurane	Which inhaled anesthetics decreases metheonine synthase activity and causes megaloblastic anemia? Nitrous oxide
Unlike inhaled anesthetics, intravenous agents such as thiopental, etomidate, and propofol - Have a faster onset and rate of recovery- Provide a state of conscious sedation- Are commonly used for induction of anesthesia	Indicate the intravenous anesthetic, which is an ultra-short-acting barbiturate Thiopental
Indicate the intravenous anesthetic, which is a benzodiazepine derivative Midazolam	Which agents is used to accelerate recovery from the sedative actions of intravenous benzodiazepines? Flumazenil

Neuroleptanalgesia has the following properties - Droperidol and fentanyl are commonly used - It can be used with nitrous oxide to provide neuroleptanesthesia - Confusion and mental depression can occur as adverse effects	**Neuroleptanalgesia has not the following properties** Hypertension is a common consequence
Which intravenous anesthetics has antiemetic actions? Propofol	**Indicate the intravenous anesthetic, which causes minimal cardiovascular and respiratory depressant effects** Etomidate
Indicate the intravenous anesthetic, which produces dissociative anesthesia Ketamine	**Following drugs directly activate the respiratory center** - Bemegride - Caffeine - Aethymizole
Following drugs do not directly activate the respiratory center Cytiton	**The mechanism of Cytiton action is** The reflex mechanism
Indicate the drug belonging to antitussives of narcotic type of action Aethylmorphine hydrochloride	**Tick out the drug belonging to non-narcotic antitussives** Tusuprex

Indicate the expectorant with the reflex mechanism Derivatives of Ipecacucnha and Thermopsis	Tick the antitussive agent with a peripheral effect Libexine
True or False. Chymotrypsin is an agent containing free sulfhydryl groups TRUE	All of these drugs contain free sulfhydryl groups - Acetylcysteine- Ambroxol- Bromhexin
The following drug do not contain free sulfhydryl groups Trypsin	Which drugs is proteolytic enzyme? Desoxiribonuclease
That drugs destroy disulfide bonds of proteoglycans, which causes depolymerization and reduction of viscosity of sputum - Acetylcysteine- Ambroxol- Bromhexin	That drugs do not destroy disulfide bonds of proteoglycans, which causes depolymerization and reduction of viscosity of sputum Desoxiribonuclease
Which of these groups of drugs is used for asthma treatment? - Methylxanthines- M-cholinoblocking agents- Beta2 - stimulants	Tick the drug belonging to non-selective beta2-adrenomimics Isoprenaline

Select the side-effect characteristic for non-selective beta2-adrenomimics Tachycardia	**Bronchodilator drug related to xanthine** Theophylline
Bronchodilator drug belonging to sympathomimics Ephedrine	**True or False. The property of prolonged theophyllines is the prevention of night asthmatic attacks.** TRUE
The mechanism of methylxanthines action is Inhibition of the enzyme phosphodiesterase	**Which M-cholinoblocking agents is used especially as an anti-asthmatic?** Ipratropium
Indicate the side effect of Theophylline Increased myocardial demands for oxygen	**The following drugs are inhaled glucocorticoids** - Triamcinolone - Beclometazone - Budesonide
The following drugs are not inhaled glucocorticoids Sodium cromoglycate	**Drug belonging to membranestabilizing agents** Sodium cromoglycate

Drug which is a 5-lipoxygenase inhibitor Zileutin	True or False. Zileutin prevents the production of leukotrienes. TRUE
Indicate the drug which is a leucotriene receptor antagonist Zafirlucast	True or False. Zafirlucast prevents aspirin-sensitive asthma. TRUE
Tick the main approach of peptic ulcer treatment - Neutralization of gastric acid- Eradication of Helicobacter pylori- Inhibition of gastric acid secretion	Gastric acid secretion is under the control of - Histamine- Acetylcholine- Gastrin
Gastric acid secretion is not under the control of Serotonin	Indicate the drug belonging to proton pump inhibitors Omeprazole
The following agents intensify the secretion of gastric glands - Gastrin- Histamine- Carbonate mineral waters	The following agent do not intensify the secretion of gastric glands Pepsin

Question	Answer
Which drugs is an agent of substitution therapy?	Hydrochloric acid
Choose the drug which is a H2-receptor antagonist	Ranitidine
The following drugs are proton pump inhibitors	- Pantoprozole - Omeprazole - Rabeprazole
Indicate the drug belonging to M1-cholinoblockers	Pirenzepin
Which drugs may cause reversible gynecomastia?	Cimetidine
True or False. Cimetidine has no effect on hepatic drug metabolism.	FALSE
Tick the drug forming a physical barrier to HCL and Pepsin	Sucralfate
Which drug is an analog of prostaglandin E1?	Misoprostole
Select the drug stimulating the protective function of the mucous barrier and the stability of the mucous membrane against damaging factors	Misoprostol
True or False. Antacids are weak bases that react with gastric hydrochloric acid to form salt and water.	TRUE

Antacids drugs	Are not Antacids drugs
- Maalox- Mylanta- Almagel	Misoprostol
Indicate the drug that cause metabolic alkalosis	Drug that causes constipation
Sodium bicarbonate	Aluminium hydroxide
The following drugs stimulate appetite	The following drugs do not stimulate appetite
- Vitamins- Bitters- Insulin	Fepranone
True or False. Ethyl alcohol is an agent decreasing appetite. FALSE	Fenfluramine An anorexigenic agent affecting serotoninergic system
The following drugs intensify gastrointestinal motility	The following drugs do not intensify gastrointestinal motility
- Metoclopramide- Domperidone- Cisapride	Papaverine

True or False. Metoclopramide is a potent dopamine antagonist. TRUE	**Emetic drug of central action** Apomorphine hydrochloride
The mechanism of Metoclopramide antiemetic action D2-dopamine and 5-HT3-serotonin receptor blocking effect	**The emetic agent having a reflex action** Ipecacuanha derivatives
The following drugs are antiemetics - Metoclopramide- Ondansetron- Chlorpromazine	**The following drugs are not antiemetics** Apomorphine hydrochloride
Indicate an antiemetic agent which is related to neuroleptics Prochlorperazine	**Drugs that reduces intestinal peristalsis** - Loperamide- Methyl cellulose- Magnesium aluminium silicate
Drugs that does not reduces intestinal peristalsis Cisapride	**Indicate the laxative drug belonging to osmotic laxatives** Sodium phosphate

The mechanism of stimulant purgatives is Increasing motility and secretion	**Drug irritating the gut and causing increased peristalsis** Phenolphthalein
The following drugs stimulate bile production and bile secretion - Cholenszyme - Oxaphenamide - Cholosas	**The following drugs do not stimulate bile production and bile secretion** Chenodiol
Stimulant of bile production of vegetable origin Cholosas	**Select the drug which inhibits peristalsis** Loperamide
The drug affecting the biliary system and relaxing Oddy sphincter No-spa	**Drugs thats stimulate erythrogenesis** - Iron dextran - Vitamine B12 - Folic acid
Drugs that does not stimulate erythrogenesis Methotrexate	**Drug that depressing erythrogenesis** Radioactive phosphorus 32

Which drug does not influence leucopoiesis? Erythropoetin	True or False. Iron deficiency anemia leads to pallor, fatigue, dizziness, exertional dyspnea and other symptoms of tissue ischemia. TRUE
Drugs used for iron deficiency anemia - Ferrous sulfate- Ferrous gluconate- Ferrous fumarate	Drugs that are not used for iron deficiency anemia Folic acid
The drug for parenteral iron therapy Fercoven	Indicate the drug which increases absorption of iron from intestine Ascorbic acid
Pernicious anemia is developed due to deficiency of Vitamin B12	Drug used for pernicious anemia Cyanocobalamin
An adverse effect of oral iron therapy is Constipation	Drug which contains cobalt atom Cyanocobalamine

Drug used in aplastic anemia Epoetin alpha	**True or False. Folic acid is recommended for treatment of megaloblastic anemia.** TRUE
Drug of granulocyte colony-stimulating factor Filgrastim	**Physiologic reactions are involved in the control of bleeding** - Platelet adhesion reaction- Platelet release reaction- Triggering of the coagulation process
Physiologic reactions that are not involved in the control of bleeding Activation of the antifibrinolytic system	**Which substances is synthesized within vessel walls and inhibits thrombogenesis?** Prostacyclin (PGI2)
The following groups of drugs are for thrombosis treatment - Anticoagulant drugs- Fibrinolitic drugs- Antiplatelet drugs	**The following group of drugs are not for thrombosis treatment** Antifibrinolitic drugs
Drug belonging to anticoagulants of direct action Heparin	**Which drugs has low-molecular weight?** Enoxaparin

Indicate the drug belonging to antagonists of heparin Protamine sulfate	**Drug used as an oral anticoagulant** Dicumarol
Drugs are indirect acting anticoagulants - Dicumarol- Warfarin- Phenindione	**Drugs that are not indirect acting anticoagulants** Dalteparin
Which drugs belongs to coumarin derivatives? Warfarin	**True or False. Heparin is effective when administred orally.** FALSE
Drugs that are antiplatelet agents - Aspirin- Ticlopidine- Clopidogrel	**Drugs that are not antiplatelet agents** Urokinase
True or False. The use of heparin is recommended for treatment of deep venous thrombosis. TRUE	**Mechanism of aspirin action is** Inhibits COX and thus thromboxane synthesis

Which doses of Aspirin may be more effective in inhibiting Tromboxane A2? (Low or High) LOW	**Which drugs is an inhibitor of platelet glycoprotein IIb/IIIa receptors?** Abciximab
True or False. Ticlopidine is an inhibitor of ADP-induced platelet aggregation. TRUE	**Which drugs is fiibrinolytic?** Streptokinase
True or False. Mechanism of urokinase action is an inhibition of Thromboxane A2. FALSE	**Fibrinolytic drugs are used for** - Central deep venous thrombosis- Multiple pulmonary emboli- Acute myocardial infarction
Fibrinolytic drugs are NOT used for Heart failure	**Indicate the drug belonging to fibrinoliytic inhibitors** Aminocapronic acid
Aminocapronic acid is a drug of choice for treatment of Bleeding from fibrinolytic therapy	**True or False. Tranexamic acid is an analog of aminocapronic acid.** TRUE

Normally involved in the pathogenesis of heart failure	Not Normally involved in the pathogenesis of heart failure
- A cardiac lesion that impairs cardiac output- An increase in peripheral vascular resistance- An increase in sodium and water retention	A decrease in preload
All of the following are compensatory mechanisms that occur during the pathogenesis of congestive heart failure	The following are not compensatory mechanisms that occur during the pathogenesis of congestive heart failure
- An increase in ventricular end-diastolic volume- An increase in the concentration of plasma catecholamines- Increased activity of the renin-angiotensin-aldosterone system	An increase in vagal tone
All of the following are recommended at the initial stages of treating patients with heart failure	The following are not recommended at the initial stages of treating patients with heart failure
- Reduced salt intake- ACE inhibitors- Diuretics	Verapamil
The following agents belong to cardiac glycosides	The following agent do not belong to cardiac glycosides
- Digoxin- Strophantin K- Digitoxin	Amrinone
The non-glycoside positive inotropic drug is	Sugar molecules in the structure of glycosides influence
Dobutamine	Pharmacokinetic properties

Aglycone is essential for Cardiotonic action	Derivative of the plant Foxglove (Digitalis) Digoxin
True or False. They inhibit the Na+/K+-ATPase and thereby increase intracellular Ca++ in myocardial cells TRUE	True or False. They cause a decrease in vagal tone FALSE
True or False. Children tolerate higher doses of digitalis than do adults TRUE	True or False. The most frequent cause of digitalis intoxication is concurrent administration of diuretics that deplete K+ TRUE
True or False. An important action of digitalis is to increase vagal tone. TRUE	True or False. Digoxin is thought to increase intracellular concentrations of calcium in myocardial cells by indirectly slowing the action of the sodium-calcium exchanger. TRUE
Compare the half-life of digoxin and the half-life of digitoxin Digitoxin is greater than digoxin	True or False about cardiac glycosides. They inhibit the activity of the Na+/K+-ATPase TRUE

True or False about cardiac glycosides. They decrease intracellular concentrations of calcium in myocytes FALSE	True or False about cardiac glycosides. They increase vagal tone TRUE
True or False about cardiac glycosides. They have a very low therapeutic index TRUE	True or False about cardiac glycosides. Digoxin is a mild inotrope TRUE
True or False about cardiac glycosides. Digoxin increases vagal tone TRUE	True or False about cardiac glycosides. Digoxin has a longer half-life than digitoxin FALSE
True or False about cardiac glycosides. Digoxin acts by inhibiting the Na+/K+ ATPase TRUE	The most cardiac manifestation of glycosides intoxication is - Atrioventricular junctional rhythm- Second-degree atrioventricular blockade- Ventricular tachycardia
The manifestations of glycosides intoxication are - Visual changes- Ventricular tachyarrhythmias- Gastrointestinal disturbances	For digitalis-induced arrhythmias the following drug is favored Lidocaine

Question	Answer
In very severe digitalis intoxication the best choice is to use	Digibind (Digoxin immune fab)
True or False about cardiac glycoside-induced ventricular tachyarrhythmias. Lidocaine is a drug of choice in treatment	TRUE
True or False about cardiac glycoside-induced ventricular tachyarrhythmias. Digibind should be used in life-threatening cases	TRUE
True or False about cardiac glycoside-induced ventricular tachyarrhythmias. They occur more frequently in patients with hyperkalemia than in those with hypokalemia	FALSE
True or False about cardiac glycoside-induced ventricular tachyarrhythmias. They are more likely to occur in patients with a severely damaged heart	TRUE
This drug is a selective beta-1 agonist	Dobutamine
Tolerance to this inotropic drug develops after a few days	Dobutamine
This drug inhibits breakdown of cAMP in vascular smooth muscle	Amrinone
This drug is useful for treating heart failure because it increases the inotropic state and reduces afterload	Amrinone
This drug acts by inhibiting type III cyclic nucleotide phosphodiesterase	Milrinone

True or False about inhibitors of type III phosphodiesterase. They raise cAMP concentrations in cardiac myocytes TRUE	True or False about inhibitors of type III phosphodiesterase. They reduce afterload TRUE
True or False about inhibitors of type III phosphodiesterase. They show significant cross-tolerance with beta-receptor agonists FALSE	True or False about inhibitors of type III phosphodiesterase. They are associated with a significant risk for cardiac arrhythmias TRUE
The following drugs are used in the treatment of severe congestive heart failure - Digoxin- Dobutamine- Dopamine	The following drug are not used in the treatment of severe congestive heart failure Verapamil
Drugs most commonly used in chronic heart failure are - Cardiac glycosides- Diuretics- Angiotensin-converting enzyme inhibitors	True or False about angiotensin converting enzyme (ACE) inhibitors. They act by inhibiting the ability of renin to convert angiotensinogen to angiotensin I. FALSE
True or False about angiotensin converting enzyme (ACE) inhibitors. Enalapril is a prodrug that is converted to an active metabolite TRUE	True or False about angiotensin converting enzyme (ACE) inhibitors. They reduce secretion of aldosterone TRUE

True or False about angiotensin converting enzyme (ACE) inhibitors. They can produce hyperkalemia in combination with a potassium-sparing diuretic TRUE	The following effects of ACE inhibitors may be useful in treating heart failure - They decrease afterload - They reduce reactive myocardial hypertrophy - They increase myocardial beta-1 adrenergic receptor density
The following effect of ACE inhibitors may be not useful in treating heart failure They increase circulating catecholamine levels	True or False about the use of angiotensin-converting enzyme (ACE) inhibitors in the treatment of heart failure. They improve hemodynamics by decreasing afterload TRUE
True or False about the use of angiotensin-converting enzyme (ACE) inhibitors in the treatment of heart failure. They can increase plasma cholesterol levels FALSE	This drug is a Class IA antiarrhythmic drug Quinidine
This drug is a Class IC antiarrhythmic drug - Lidocaine - Flecainide	This drug is a Class II antiarrhythmic drug Propranolol
This drug is a Class III antiarrhythmic drug Sotalol	This drug prolongs repolarization Sotalol

This drug is a Class IV antiarrhythmic drug Verapamil	This drug is used in treating supraventricular tachycardias Digoxin
This drug is associated with Torsades de pointes Sotalol	This drug has beta-adrenergic blocking activity Sotalol
This drug is useful in terminating atrial but not ventricular tachycardias Verapamil	This is a drug of choice for acute treatment of ventricular tachycardias Lidocaine
True or False. The calcium channel blockers have direct negative inotropic effects because they reduce the inward movement of calcium during the action potential. TRUE	True or False. Common unwanted effects of the dihydropyridines are due to vasodilation. TRUE
True or False. Verapamil is a more potent vasodilator than nifedipine. FALSE	This drug is contraindicated in patients with moderate to severe heart failure Verapamil

This drug is used intravenously to terminate supraventricular tachycardias Verapamil	This drug has a little or no direct effect on chronotropy and dromotropy at normal doses Nifedipine
True or False. Verapamil has a significant effect on automaticity in the SA node. TRUE	This drug acts by inhibiting slow calcium channels in the SA and AV nodes Diltiazem
True or False about verapamil. It blocks L-type calcium channels TRUE	True or False about verapamil. It increases heart rate FALSE
True or False about verapamil. It relaxes coronary artery smooth muscle TRUE	True or False about verapamil. It depresses cardiac contractility TRUE
The following calcium channel blockers are useful in the treatment of cardiac arrhythmias - Bepridil- Diltiazem- Verapamil	The following calcium channel blockers are not useful in the treatment of cardiac arrhythmias Nifedipine

The following are common adverse effects of calcium channel blockers - Dizziness- Headache- Flushing	**The following are not common adverse effects of calcium channel blockers** Skeletal muscle weakness
The adverse reactions characteristic for lidocaine Hypotension, paresthesias, convulsions	**True or False about nitrate mechanism of action. Therapeutically active agents in this group are capable of releasing nitric oxide (NO) in to vascular smooth muscletarget tissues.** TRUE
True or False about nitrate mechanism of action. Nitric oxide (NO) is an effective activator of soluble guanylyl cyclase and probably acts mainly through this mechanism TRUE	**Which nitrates and nitrite drugs are long-acting?** Sustac
Which nitrates and nitrite drugs is a short-acting drug? Amyl nitrite, inhalant (Aspirols, Vaporole)	**Which nitrates and nitrite drugs is used for prevention of angina attack?** - Nitroglycerin, 2% ointment (Nitrol)- Nitroglycerin, oral sustained-release (Nitrong)- Isosorbide mononitrate (Ismo)
Duration of nitroglycerin action (sublingual) is 10-30 minutes	**True or False about the mechanism of nitrate beneficial clinical effect. Decreased myocardial oxygen requirement** TRUE

True or False about the mechanism of nitrate beneficial clinical effect. Relief of coronary artery spasm TRUE	True or False about the mechanism of nitrate beneficial clinical effect. Improved perfusion to ischemic myocardium TRUE
True or False about the mechanism of nitrate beneficial clinical effect. Increased myocardial oxygen consumption FALSE	Side effect of nitrates and nitrite drugs are - Orthostatic hypotension, tachycardia - Throbbing headache - Tolerance
True or False about mechanism of calcium channel blockers' action. Calcium channel blockers bind to L-type calcium channel sites TRUE	Which antianginal agents is a calcium channel blocker? Nifedipine
Which cardiovascular system effects refers to a calcium channel blocker? - The reduction of peripheral vascular resistance - The reduction of cardiac contractility and, in some cases, cardiac output - Relief of coronary artery spasm	Main clinical use of calcium channel blockers is - Angina pectoris - Hypertension - Supraventricular tachyarrhythmias
Which antianginal agents is a myotropic coronary dilator Dipyridamole	Which antianginal agents is a beta-adrenoceptor-blocking drug Atenolol

The following agents are cardioselective beta1-adrenoceptor-blocking drugs labeled for use in angina

- Metoprolol- Talinolol- Atenolol | The following agents are not cardioselective beta1-adrenoceptor-blocking drugs labeled for use in angina

Propranolol |
| True or False about beta-adrenoceptor-blocking drugs. These agents has a moderate reflex and vascular dilative action caused by the stimulation of sensitive nerve endings

TRUE | Which antianginal agents refers to reflex coronary dilators:

Validol |
| True or False about Validol. Validol has a moderate reflex and vascular dilative action caused by the stimulation of sensitive nerve endings

TRUE | True or False about Validol. At sublingual administration the effect is produced in five minutes and 70 % of the preparation is released in 3 minutes

TRUE |
| True or False about Validol. It is used in cases of angina pectoris, motion sickness, nausea, vomiting when seasick or airsick and headaches due to taking nitrates

TRUE | Which antianginal agents is the specific bradycardic drug

Alinidine |
| True or False about Alinidine. Bradycardic drugs have a moderate reflex and vascular dilative action caused by the stimulation of sensitive nerve endings

FALSE | True or False about Alinidine. The predominant effect of bradycardic drugs is a decrease in heart rate without significant changes in arterial pressure

TRUE |

True or False about Alinidine. The protective effect of bradycardic drugs is likely due to a reduced O2 demand TRUE	True or False about Alinidine. Specific bradycardic agents are used in the management of a wide range of cardiovascular disorders, including sinus tachyarrhythmias and angina TRUE
True or False about Dipyridamole. Dipyridamole is an agent that blocks the reabsorption and breakdown of adenosine that results in an increase of endogenous adenosine and TRUE	True or False about Dipyridamole. The drug causes relative hypoperfusion of myocardial regions served by coronary arteries with haemodynamically significant stenoses TRUE
True or False about Dipyridamole. Dipyridamole is a platelet aggregation inhibitor TRUE	Which antianginal agents is a potassium channel opener Minoxidil
True or False about potassium channel openers. These agents has a moderate reflex and vascular dilative action caused by the stimulation of sensitive nerve endings FALSE	This drug reduces blood pressure by acting on vasomotor centers in the CNS Clonidine
The following are central acting antihypertensive drugs - Methyldopa- Clonidine- Moxonidine	A ganglioblocking drug for hypertension treatment is Trimethaphan

A sympatholythic drug Guanethidine	Drug with nonselective beta-adrenoblocking activity Propranolol
The selective blocker of beta-1 adrenoreceptors Atenolol	An alpha and beta adrenoreceptors blocker Labetalol
This drug inhibits the angiotensin-converting enzyme - Captopril- Enalapril- Ramipril	This drug is a directly acting vasodilator Nifedipine
Diuretic agent for hypertension treatment Dichlothiazide	This drug blocks alpha-1 adrenergic receptors Prazosin
This drug activates alpha-2 adrenergic receptors Clonidine	This drug is an inhibitor of renin synthesis Propranolol

This drug is a non-peptide angiotensin II receptor antagonist Losartan	This drug is a potassium channel activator Diazoxide
True or False about angiotensin II. It is a peptide hormone TRUE	True or False about angiotensin II. It stimulates the secretion of aldosterone TRUE
True or False about angiotensin II. Angiotensin I is almost as potent as angiotensin II FALSE	True or False about angiotensin II. It is a potent vasoconstrictor TRUE
This drug is contraindicated in patients with bronchial asthma Propranolol	This drug is converted to an active metabolite after absorption Enalapril
This drug routinely produces some tachycardia Nifedipine	True or False about vasodilators. Hydralazine causes tachycardia TRUE

True or False about vasodilators. Nifedipine is a dopamine receptor antagonist FALSE	True or False about vasodilators. Nitroprusside dilates both arterioles and veins TRUE
True or False about vasodilators. Minoxidil can cause hypertrichosis TRUE	True or False about verapamil. It blocks L-type calcium channels TRUE
True or False about verapamil. It increases heart rate FALSE	True or False about verapamil. It relaxes coronary artery smooth muscle TRUE
True or False about verapamil. It depresses cardiac contractility TRUE	Unwanted effects of clonidine Sedative and hypnotic effects
The reason of beta-blockers administration for hypertension treatment is Decreasing of heart work	An endogenous vasoconstrictor that can stimulate aldosterone release from suprarenal glands Angiotensin II

The group of antihypertensive drugs which diminishes the metabolism of bradykinin Angiotensin-converting enzyme inhibitors	**Hydralazine (a vasodilator) can produce** Tachycardia, lupus erhythromatosis
Vasodilator which releases NO Sodium nitroprusside	**The reason of diuretics administration for hypertension treatment is** Diminishing of blood volume and amount of Na+ ions in the vessels endothelium
Diuretic agent – aldosterone antagonist Spironolactone	**Diuretic agent having a potent and rapid effect** Furosemide
The main principle of shock treatment is To improve the peripheral blood flow	**Drug which increases cardiac output** Noradrenalin
The synthetic vasoconstrictor having an adrenomimic effect Phenylephrine	**Indicate the vasoconstrictor of endogenous origin** Angiotensinamide

Which type of receptors can be activated by angiotensinamide Angiotensin's receptors	General unwanted effects of vasoconstrictors is Decrease of peripheral blood flow
For increasing blood pressure in case of low cardiac output the following agents must be used Positive inotropic drugs	Positive inotropic drug of glycoside structure Digoxin
Positive inotropic drug of non-glycoside structure Dobutamine	Dopamine at low doses influences mainly Dopamine receptors (leads to vasodilation of renal and mesenterial vessels)
Dopamine at medium doses influences mainly Beta-1 adrenoreceptors (leads to enhanced cardiac output)	Dopamine in high doses influences mainly the Alfa-adrenoreceptors (leads to peripheral vasoconstriction)
Group of drugs for treatment of shock with hypovolaemia (reduced circulating blood volume) Plasmoexpanders	Group of drugs for chronic hypotension treatment Analeptics and tonics

Indicate the group of drugs influencing the cerebral flow - Ca-channel blockers- Derivatives of GABA- Derivatives of Vinca minor plant	**Grug influencing the blood flow which is related to antiplatelet agents** Aspirin
Which drugs is related to anticoagulants and may be useful in disorders of cerebral circulation? Heparin	**Indicate the drugs which are Ca-channel blockers influencing the brain blood flow** Nimodipine, Cinnarizine
Indicate the drugs influencing the blood flow in the brain - derivatives of GABA Aminalon, Picamilon	**Indicate the drug - Vinca minor alcaloid** Vinpocetine
Drug – a derivative of Ergot Nicergoline	**Indicate the nootropic agent useful in disorders of brain circulation** Pyracetam
What is the main action of GABA derivatives in disorders of brain circulation? Stimulation of the metabolic processes in neurons	**Appropriate mechanism of vinpocetine action** It dilates cerebral vessels and improves blood supply

Antiaggregants are used in disorders of brain circulation for Improving the microcirculation in cerebral tissue	Migraine is a disorder connected with Dysfunction of regulation of cerebral vessel tonus
True or False. Main agents for acute migraine attack treatment are Ergot and indol derivatives and NSAID's. TRUE	The following Indol derivative is used for treatment of acute migraine attack Sumatriptan
The following Ergot derivative is used for treatment of acute migraine attack Ergotamine	The derivative of lysergic acid for migraine attack prevention is Methysergide
Hormones are Products of endocrine gland secretion	An endocrine drug which is an amino acid derivative Thyroxine
An endocrine drug which is a peptide derivative Oxitocin	An endocrine drug which is a steroidal derivative Hydrocortisone

Hormone analogues are Synthetic compounds, which resemble the naturally occurring hormones	True or False about mechanism of action of hormones. Hormones interact with the specific receptors in the wall of the cells FALSE
True or False about mechanism of action of hormones. Cyclic AMP acts as a second messenger system TRUE	True or False about mechanism of action of hormones. They stimulate adenylcyclase enzyme TRUE
True or False about mechanism of action of hormones. Many hormones owe their effect to primary actions on subcellular membrane. TRUE	Hypothalamic and pituitary hormones (and their synthetic analogs) have pharmacologic applications in three areas, excet As food supplements
Which hormones is produced by the hypothalamic gland? Growth hormone-releasing hormone (GHRH)	Which hormones is produced by the anterior lobe of the pituitary? Growth hormone (somatotropin, GH)
The posterior pitutary does NOT secret Growth hormone	The posterior pitutary secret - Vasopressin- Oxytocin

Which organs is a target for prolactin? Mammary gland	**Which organ hormones is a target for growth hormone (somatotropine, GH)?** Insulin-like growth factors (IGF, somatomedins)
True or False about growth hormone. It may stimulate the synthesis or release of somatomedins TRUE	**True or False about growth hormone. Low levels of insulin-like growth factor (IGF)-1 are associated with dwarfism** TRUE
True or False about growth hormone. Hypersecretion can result in acromegaly FALSE	**True or False about growth hormone. It is contraindicated in subjects with closed epiphyses** TRUE
adrenocorticotropic hormone (ACTH) include - Endogenous ACTH is also called corticotropin- ACTH stimulates the synthesis of corticosteroids- ACTH is most useful clinically as a diagnostic tool in adrenal insufficiency	**adrenocorticotropic hormone (ACTH) do not include** The oral route is the preferred rout of administration
True or False. The hypothalamic control exists for the thyroid gland. TRUE	**Indications of bromocriptine are** - Prolactin-secreting adenomas- Amenorrhea-Galactorrhea- Acromegaly

Indications of bromocriptine are not Prolactin deficiency	**Currently used dopamine agonists decreasing pituitary prolactin secretion are following** - Bromocriptine - Cabergoline - Pergolide
Indications of oxitocin are - Labor and augment dysfunctional labor for conditions requiring early vaginal delivery - Incompleted abortion - For control of pospartum uterine hemorrhage	**Indications of vasopressin are** Pituitary diabetes insipidus
Vasopressin possesses the following Antidiuretic property	**Oxytocin produces the following effects** - It causes contraction of the uterus - It assists the progress of spermatozoa into the uterine cavity - It brings about milk ejection from the lactating mammary gland
Vasopressin causes a pressor effect by A direct action on smooth muscles of the blood vessels	**True or False. Hypothyroidism is a syndrome resulting from deficiency of thyroid hormones and is manifested largely by a reversible slowing down of all body functions** TRUE
Which hormones is produced by the thyroid gland? Thyroxine	**Which hormones is produced by the thyroid gland?** Triiodothyronine

Thyroid stimulating hormone regulates the following - Iodine uptake- Biosynthesis of iodothyroglobulin- Release of thyroid hormone into the plasma	**True or False about Thyroid hormones. Decline of the basal metabolic rate in the body** FALSE
True or False about Thyroid hormones. Increase in the rate and force of contraction of the heart TRUE	**True or False about Thyroid hormones. Increase in the blood cholestrol level** TRUE
True or False about Thyroid hormones. Increase in the heat production TRUE	**Synthesis and release of thyroid hormones are controlled by** - Anterior pituitary alone- Hypothalamus alone- Blood levels of thyroid hormones alone
Thyrotrophin stimulates Release of thyroxine and triidothyronine	**The rate of secretion of thyrotropin is controlled by** The concentration of thyroid hormones in blood
Indications of thyroid hormones are - Cretinism- Myxoedema- Hashimoto's disease	**The common side effect of thyroid hormones is** Exopthalmos

Currently used antithyroid drugs include the following	**In an area where goitre is endemic, which of the following drugs is used?**
- Propylthiouracil (PTU)- Diatrizoate sodium (Hypaque)- Methimazole (Tapazole)	Iodide 1 part in 100000
Iodide preparations can be used in following situations	**Iodide preparations can not be used in following situations**
- In thyroid disorders- In granulomatous lesions e.g. Syphilis- As an antiseptic	In iodism
Daily administration of large doses (several milligrammes) of iodides to a thyrotoxic patient causes	**Radioiodines (I131 and I132) is suitable for**
Thyroid gland growing firm and less vascular	Elderly patients (over 45 years)
Radioiodines in the body emit	**Secretory products of pancreatic β-cells are**
Mainly β radiations	Insulin, C-peptide, proinsulin, islet amyloid polypeptide (IAPP)
Insulin is	**Insulin is a polypeptide hence**
A small protein with a molecular weight of 5808 having disulphide linkage	It is destroyed by gastric juice

True or False. Bovine insulin is less antigenic than porcine. FALSE	Insulin causes reduction in blood sugar level by the following mechanisms - Increased glucose uptake in the peripheral tissue- Reduction of breakdown of glycogen- Diminished gluconeogenesis
True or False about glucagon. Stimulates gluconeogenesis in the liver TRUE	Insulin can not be administered by Oral route
Sources of human insulin production are Recombinant DNA techniques by inserting the proinsulin gene into E. coli or yeast	The primary reason for a physician to prescribe human insulin is that It can be given to patients who have an allergy to animal insulins
True or False about crystalline zinc (regular) insulin. It can serve as replacement therapy for juvenile-onset diabetes TRUE	True or False about crystalline zinc (regular) insulin. It can be administered intravenously TRUE
True or False about crystalline zinc (regular) insulin. It is a short-acting insulin TRUE	True or False about crystalline zinc (regular) insulin. It can be administered orally FALSE

Diabetic coma is treated by the administration of Crystalline insulin	Sulphonylureas act by Stimulating the beta islet cells of pancreas to produce insulin
True or False. Sulphonylureas are effective in totally insulin deficient patients. FALSE	Currently used second-generation sulfonylureas include - Glyburide (Glibenclamide)- Glipizide (Glydiazinamide)- Glimepiride (Amaril)
Currently used oral hypoglycemic thiazolidinediones include - Pioglitazone (Actos)- Rosiglitazone (Avandia)	Thiazolidinediones act by Diminishing insulin resistance by increasing glucose uptake and metabolism in muscle and adipose tissues
Currently used alpha-glucosidase inhibitors include - Acarbose (Precose)- Miglitol (Glyset)- All of the above	Alpha-glucosidase inhibitors act by Competitive inhibiting of intestinal alpha-ghucosidases and modulating the postprandial digestion and absorption of starch and disaccharides
Potency of action of Miglitol is six times higher than that of acarbose	Which oral hypoglycaemic drugs stimulates both synthesis and release of insulin from beta islet cells Glibenclamide

Currently used oral hypoglycemic biguanides include - Repaglinide (Prandin)- Metformin- Phenformine	**The action of insulin is potentiated by** Biguanides
Duration of action of Chlorpropamide is more than that of tolbutamide	**True or False. Side effects of sulphonylureas are less than those of biguanides.** TRUE
Biguanides are used in In case of hyperglycemic shock	**Which agents is/are important hormonal antagonists of insulin in the body?** - Glucagon- Adrenal steroids- Adrenaline
Glucagon is A peptide – identical in all mammals – consisting of a single chain of 29 amino acids.	**True or False. Glucagon is synthesized in the A cells of the pancreatic islets of Langerhans.** TRUE
True or False. Glucagon is a peptide – identical in all mammals – consisting of a single chain of 29 amino acids TRUE	**True or False. Glucagon is extensively degraded in the liver and kidney as well as in plasma, and at its tissue receptor sites.** TRUE

True or False. Half-life of glucagon is between 6 and 8 hours, which is similar to that of insulin. FALSE	Glucagon can be used in - Severe hypoglycemia- Endocrine diagnosis- Beta-blocker poisoning
Main complications of insulin therapy include - Hypoglycemia- Insulin allergy- Lipodystrophy at an injection site	The major natural estrogens produced by women are - Estradiol (Estradiol-17β, E2)- Estron (E1)- Estriol (E3)
True or False. Estrogens are required for normal sexual maturation and growth of the female TRUE	True or False. Estrogens decrease the rate of resorption of bone TRUE
True or False. Estrogens enhance the coagulability of blood TRUE	The major synthetic estrogens are - Dienestrol- Diethylstilbestrol- Benzestrol
True or False about estrogens. Estradiol binds strongly to an α2-globulin and albumin with lower affinity TRUE	True or False about estrogens. Estrone and estriol have lower affinity for the estrogen receptors than estradiol TRUE

Indications of synthetic estrogens are - Primary hypogonadism- Postmenopausal hormonal therapy- Hormonal contraception	**Main complications of estrogens' therapy include** - Postmenopausal uterine bleeding- Breast tenderness- Hyperpigmentation
Main contraindications of estrogens' therapy include - Estrogen-dependent neoplasmas such as carcinoma of the endometrium or carcinoma of the breast- Undiagnosed genital bleeding- Liver disease	**Tamoxifen is** Antiestrogen
Progesterone is secreted by Corpus luteum	**The major natural progestin is** Progesterone
True or False about progestins. Progesterone is rapidly absorbed following administration by any route TRUE	True or False about progestins. In the liver, progesterone is metabolized to pregnanediol and conjugated with glucuronic acid. TRUE
True or False about progestins. Significant amounts of progestins and their metabolites are excreted in the urine TRUE	True or False. The normal ovary produces small amount of androgens, including testosterone, androstenedione, and degydroepiandrosterone. TRUE

Noncontraceptive clinical uses of progestins are - Hormone replacement therapy- Dysmenorrhea- Endometriosis	True or False. Estrogens possess immunomodulator properties, but progestins do immunodepressant ones. TRUE
Mifepristone (RU-486) is Antiprogestin	True or False. Mifepristone (RU-486) is used as a contraceptive and abortifacient. TRUE
True or False about oral contraceptives. The "combination pill" contains both estrogen and progestin TRUE	True or False about oral contraceptives. Ethinyl estradiol and mestranol are commonly used in oral contraceptives TRUE
True or False about oral contraceptives. The "minipill" contains progestin alone TRUE	True or False about oral contraceptives. The "triphasic pill" contains estrogen, progestin, and luteinizing hormine (LH) FALSE
Glucocorticoids are hormonal steroids Having an important effect on intermediary metabolism, cardiovascular function, growth, and immunity	Inflammation is A localized protective reaction of a tissue to irritation, injury, or infection, characterized by pain, redness, swelling, and sometimes loss of function

An acute, transient phase, of inflammation is characterized by Local vasodilatation and increased capillary permeability (phase of damage)	**A delayed, subacute phase, of inflammation is characterized by** Infiltration of leucocytes and phagocytic cells (phase of exudation)
A chronic, proliferative phase, of inflammation is characterized by Tissue degeneration and fibrosis occurrence (phase of proliferation)	**The following substances are considered to be referred to as eicosanoids** - Prostaglandins - Leukotrienes - Thromboxanes
True or False about cortisol (hydrocortisone). Cortisol is synthesized from cholesterol TRUE	True or False about cortisol (hydrocortisone). ACTH governs cortisol secretion TRUE
True or False about cortisol (hydrocortisone). Most cortisol is inactivated in the liver TRUE	True or False about cortisol (hydrocortisone). The half-life of cortisol in the circulations is normally about 60-90 hours. FALSE
True or False about glucocorticoids. Effects of glucocorticoids are mediated by widely distributed glucocorticoid receptors that are members of the superfamily of nuclear receptors. TRUE	True or False about glucocorticoids. Glucocorticoids have dose-related metabolic effects on carbohydrate, protein, and fat metabolism. TRUE

True or False about glucocorticoids. Glucocorticoids have pro-inflammatory effects. FALSE	True or False about glucocorticoids. Glucocorticoids have catabolic effects in lymphoid and connective tissue, muscle, fat, and skin. TRUE
Which glucocorticoids is a short- to medium-acting drug? Prednisolon	Which glucocorticoids is an intermediate-acting drug? Triamcinolone
Which glucocorticoids is a long-acting drug? Dexamethasone	Which glucocorticoids have one fluoride atom in its chemical structure? Triamcinolone
Which glucocorticoids have two fluoride atoms in its chemical structure? Fluocinolone	Which glucocorticoids has no fluoride atoms in its chemical structure? Prednisolon
Anti-inflammatory effect of glucocorticoids is caused by - Reducing the prostaglandin and leukotriene which results from inhibition of phospholipase A2- Reducing macrophages migration into the site of inflammation- Decreasing capillary permeability	True or False about anti-inflammatory effect of glucocorticoids. Anti-inflammatory effect of glucocorticoids results from inhibition of cyclooxygenase FALSE

Immunosupressive effect of glucocorticoids is caused by	True or False about anti-inflammatory effect of NSAIDs. Anti-inflammatory effect of NSAIDs results from inhibition of cyclooxygenase
Reducing concentration of lymphocytes (T and B cells) and inhibiting function of tissue macrophages andother antigen-presenting cells	TRUE
True or False about anti-inflammatory effect of NSAIDs. Anti-inflammatory effect of NSAIDs results from inhibition of phospholipase A2 and reducing prostaglandin andleukotriene synthesis	Serious side effects of glucocorticoids include
FALSE	- Acute peptic ulcers- Iatrogenic Cushing's syndrome (rounding, puffiness, fat deposition and plethora alter the appearance of the face – moon faces)- Hypomania or acute psychosis
Serious side effects of glucocorticoids include	True or False. Selective COX-2 inhibitors are safer than nonselective COX-1 inhibitors but without loss of efficacy.
- Adrenal suppression- Insomnia, behavioral changes (primarily hypomania)- Rounding, puffiness, fat deposition and plethora alter the appearance of the face – moon faces	TRUE
True or False. The constitutive COX-2 isoform tends to be homeostatic in function, while COX-1 is induced during inflammation and tends to facilitate the inflammatory response.	Which property combinations is peculiar to the majority of NSAIDs?
FALSE	Antipyretic, analgesic, anti-inflammatory
Which NSAIDs is a propionic acid derivative?	Which NSAIDs is an indol derivative?
Ibuprofen	Indomethacin

Which NSAIDs is a pyrazolone derivative? Metamizole (Analgin)	**Which NSAIDs is a fenamate derivative?** Meclofenamic acid
Which NSAIDs is an oxicam derivative? Piroxicam	**Which NSAIDs is a selective COX-2 inhibitor?** Celecoxib
Which NSAIDs is a nonselective COX inhibitor Piroxicam	**True or False. Aspirin inhibits phospholipase A2** TRUE
Side effects of aspirin include - Gastric upset (intolerance)- Salicylism (vomiting, tinnitus, decreased hearing, and vertigo)- Gastric ulcers and upper gastrointestinal bleeding	**Serious side effects of metamizole (analgin) include** Agranulocytosis, aplastic anemia
Side effects of indometacin include - Abdominal pain, diarrhea, gastrointestinal hemorrhage and pancreatitis- Dizziness, confusion and depression- Trombocytopenia	**True or False. Ketoprofen is a propionic acid derivative that inhibits both cyclooxygenase (nonselectively) and lipoxygenase.** TRUE

True or False. Ketorolac is an NSAID that is promoted for systemic use as an anti-inflammatory, not as an analgesic drug. FALSE	**Which drugs is a 5-lipoxygenase (5-LOG) inhibitor?** Zileuton (Zyflo)
Which drugs is a leucotreine D4 receptor (LTD4) blocker? Zafirleukast (Accolate)	**Which drugs is a thromboxane A2 receptor (TXA2) antagonist?** Sulotroban
Adaptive (acquired) immunity refers to Antigen-specific defense mechanisms that take several days to become protective and are designed to react with and remove a specific antigen. This is the immunity one develops throughout life	**Allergic reaction is** A local or generalized reaction of an organism to internal or external contact with a specific allergen to which the organism has been previously sensitized
Immediate allergy reaction (type I allergic reaction) is An allergic or immune response that begins within a period lasting from a few minutes to about an hour after exposure to an antigen to which the individual has been sensitized	**Delayed allergy reaction (type IV allergic reaction) is** An allergic reaction that becomes apparent only hours after contact
Immunodeficiency A disorder or deficiency of the normal immune response	**H1 histamine receptor subtype is distributed in** Smooth muscle, endothelium and brain

H2 histamine receptor subtype is distributed in Gastric mucosa, cardiac muscle, mast cells and brain	**Most tissue histamine is sequestered and bound in** - Granules in mast cells or basophils - Cell bodies of histaminergic neurons - Enterochromaffin-like cell of the fondus of the stomach
These categories of histamine H1 antagonists are noted for sedative effects - Ethanolamines (aminoalkyl ethers), i.e. Dimedrol, Clistin - Ethylenediamines, i.e. Suprastine - Phenothiazines, i.e. Diprazine, Promethazine	**Which category of histamine H1 antagonists is noted for the best antiemetic action?** Ethanolamines (aminoalkyl ethers), i.e. Doxylamine
These categories of histamine H1 antagonists are noted for the anticholinergic effect - Alkylamines (propylamines), i.e. Brompheniramine - Ethylenediamines, i.e. Suprastine - Phenothiazines, i.e. Diprazine, Promethazine	**Which category of histamine H1 antagonists is noted for the alpha-adrenoreceptor-blocking effect?** Phenothiazines, i.e. Diprazine, Promethazine
Which category of histamine H1 antagonists is noted for the highest local anesthetic effect? Phenothiazines, i.e. Promethazine	**Which category of histamine H1 antagonists is recognized for as second-generation antihistamines?** Piperidines, i.e. Loratadine, Fexofenadine
These histamine H1 antagonists are recognized for as second-generation antihistamines - Astemizole - Loratadine (Claritin) - Cetirizine (Zyrtec)	**Which of histamine H1 antagonists is noted for the serotonin-blocking effect?** Cyproheptadine

Which histamine H1 antagonists is a long-acting (up to 24-48 h) antihistamine drug? Diazoline	Which of histamine H1 antagonists is noted for the ulcerogenic effect? Diazoline
Indication for administration of histamine H1 antagonists is - Prevention or treatment of the symptoms of allergic reactions (rhinitis, urticaria)- Motion sickness and vestibular disturbances- Nausea and vomiting in pregnancy ("morning sickness")	Indications for administration of histamine H1 antagonists are - Prevention or treatment of the symptoms of allergic reactions (rhinitis, urticaria)- Nausea and vomiting in pregnancy ("morning sickness")- Treatment of sleep disorders
Side effect of first-generation histamine H1 antagonists is Sedation	Immunosupressive effect of glucocorticoids is caused by Reducing concentration of lymphocytes (T and B cells) and inhibiting function of tissue macrophages andother antigen-presenting cells
The Immunosuppressive agent is - Corticosteroids- Cyclosporine- Tacrolimus (FK 506)	Class of cyclosporine A is Immunosuppressive agents
Mechanism of action of cyclosporine A is Inhibits calcineurin	Side effect of cyclosporine A is - Tremor- GI disturbance- Hepatotoxicity

Side effect of cyclosporine A is Tremor	**Side effect of cyclosporine A is** GI disturbance
Indication of cyclosporine A is Idiopathic nephrotic syndrome	**Half-life of cyclosporine A is** 19 hours
Class of I.V. IgG preparation is Immunoglobulins	**Mechanism of action of I.V. IgG preparation is** Compete for Fc receptors with autoantibodies
Half-life of I.V. IgG preparation is: 21 days	**Indication for I.V. IgG preparation administration is** Prophylaxis of certain infections
Cytotoxic agents are - Azathioprine- Leflunomide- Cyclophosphamide	**Class of sirolimus (rapamycin) is** Immunosuppressive agents

Mechanism of action of sirolimus (rapamycin) is Inhibits calcineurin	**Monoclonal antibodies is** - Trastuzumab - Rituximab - OKT-3
Class of OKT-3 is Monoclonal antibodies	**Half-life of OKT-3 is** 18-24 hours
The indication for interferon gamma administration is Chronic granulomatous disease	**The side effect of interferon gamma is** Fatigue
Half-life of interferon gamma is 25-35 minutes	**Half-life of interferon alpha is** 4-16 hours
The indication for interferon alpha administration is - Hepatitis C virus infection - Kaposi's sarcoma - Condyloma acuminatum	**Class of tacrolimus (FK-506) is** Immunosuppressive agents

Mechanism of action of tacrolimus (FK-506) is Inhibits calcineurin	**Immunomodulating agent is** Levamisole
Immunomodulating agents are Tacrolimus (FK-506)	**Mechanism of action of levamisole is** Increase the number of T-cells
Vitamins are Any of various fat-soluble or water-soluble organic substances essential in minute amounts for normal growth and activity of the body and obtained naturally from plant and animal fo	**Vitamin-like compounds are** A number of compounds, whose nutritional requirements exist at specific periods of development, particularly neonatal development, and periods of rapid growth
Antivitamins are Substances that prevent vitamins from exerting their typical metabolic effects	**Coenzymes are** Nonprotein organic substances that usually contain a vitamin or mineral and combines with a specific apoenzyme to form an active enzyme system
Antienzymes are Agents, especially an inhibitory enzymes or an antibodies to enzymes, that retard, inhibit, or destroy enzymic activity	**True or False. Hypovitaminosis is an insufficiency of one or more essential vitamins.** TRUE

Select a fat-soluble vitamin Tocopherol	Select a water-soluble vitamin Vitamin B1
Which vitamins can be also synthesized from a dietary precursor? Vitamin A	Which vitamins resembles with hormone Vitamin D
Beri-beri is caused by the deficiency of Thiamine	True or False about vitamin A functions. Retinoic acid is especially important during embryogenesis TRUE
True or False about vitamin A functions. Acts as a hormone involved in regulation of calcium and phosphorus homeostasis FALSE	Xerophthalmia is Extreme dryness of the conjunctiva resulting from a disease localized in the eye or from systemic deficiency of vitamin A
Keratomalacia is: A condition, usually in children with vitamin A deficiency, characterized by softening and subsequent ulceration and perforation of the cornea	Night blindness (Hemeralopia, Nyctalopia) is A condition of the eyes in which vision is normal in daylight or other strong light but is abnormally weak or completely lost at night or in dim light and that results from vitamin A deficiency

True or False about vitamin E functions. Antisterility and antiabortion factor TRUE	True or False about vitamin E functions. Specifically required for synthesis of prothrombin and several other clotting factors FALSE
True or False about vitamin E functions. An essential for oxidative processes regulation TRUE	True or False about vitamin B1. An essential coenzyme for oxidative decarboxylate of alpha-keto acids, most important being conversion of pyruvate to acetyl coenzyme A TRUE
True or False about vitamin B2 functions. Essential constituent of flavoproteins, flavin mononucleotide (FMN) and flavin adenine dinucleotide (FAD) TRUE	True or False about vitamin B2 functions. Plays key roles in hydrogen transfer reactions associated with glycolysis, TCA cycle and oxidative phosphorylation TRUE
True or False about vitamin B2 functions. An essential coenzyme for oxidative decarboxylate of alpha-keto acids, most important being conversion of pyruvate to acetyl coenzyme A FALSE	True or False about vitamin B2 functions. Deficiency symptoms are cheilitis, cheilosis and angular stomatitis TRUE
True or False about vitamin PP (B3, niacin) functions. Active group of the coenzymes nicotinamide-adenine dinucleotide (NAD) and nicotinamide-adenine phosphate (NADP) TRUE	True or False about pantothinic acid functions. Essential constituent of coenzyme A, the important coenzyme for acyl transfer in the TCA cycle and de novo fatty acid synthesis TRUE

True or False about vitamin C functions. Has antioxidant properties and is required for various hydroxylation reactions e.g. proline to hydroxypoline for collagen synthesis TRUE	Dermatitis, diarrhoea and dementia are characteristics of Pellagra
Pellagra is A disease caused by a deficiency of niacin in the diet and characterized by skin eruptions, digestive and nervous system disturbances, and eventual mental deterioration	Rickets is A deficiency disease resulting from a lack of vitamin D or calcium and from insufficient exposure to sunlight, characterized by defective bone growth and occurring chiefly in children
Scurvy is A disease caused by deficiency of vitamin C and characterized by spongy bleeding gums, bleeding under the skin, and weakness	Which vitamins is given along with isoniazide in treatment of tuberculosis? Pyridoxine
Which vitamins is also known as an antisterility factor? Vitamin E	Mega doses of which vitamin are some time beneficial viral respiratory infections Vitamin C
Which vitamins improves megaloblast anemia but does not protect the neurological manifestations of pernicious anemia? Vitamin B12	True or False. Vitamin K enhances the anticoagulant property of coumarins. FALSE

Loosening of teeth, gingivitis and hemorrhage occur in the deficiency of Vitamin C	**Ingestion of polar bear liver may cause acute poisoning of** Vitamin A
Which antivitamins prevent a vitamin B6 from exerting its typical metabolic effects? - Isoniazide- Ethanol- Carbamazepine	**Which antivitamins prevent a vitamin A from exerting its typical metabolic effects?** Lipooxidase
Which antivitamins prevent a vitamin K from exerting its typical metabolic effects? - Cholestiramine- Coumarins- Antibiotics	**Which coenzymes is of vitamin origin?** Piridixal-5-phosphate
Which coenzymes is not of vitamin origin? - Coenzyme Q10- Magnesium- Carnitine	**These substances are vitamin-like compounds** - Choline- Vitamin U (methylmethioninesulfonil chloride)- Orotate acid
Which substances is a vitamin-like compound? Taurine	**Which antienzymes is a proteolysis inhibitor?** Contrical

Which antienzymes is a beta-lactamase inhibitor? - Clavulanic acid - Sulbactam - Tazobactam	**Which antienzymes is a fibrinolysis inhibitor?** Aminocaproic acid
Which antienzymes is an aldehyde dehydrogenase inhibitor? Disulfiram	**Which antienzymes is a cholinesterase inhibitor?** Physostigmine
Which antienzymes is a monoamine oxidase (MAO) inhibitor Selegiline	**Which antienzymes is a xantine oxidase inhibitor?** Allopurinol
Which antienzymes is an aromatase inhibitor used in cancer therapy? Aminoglutethimide	**Which enzymes improves GIT functions (replacement therapy)** Pepsin
Which enzymes has fibrinolytic activity? Urokinase	**Which enzymes is used in cancer therapy?** L-asparaginase

True or False about nutritional supplement (dietary supplement). Nutritional supplements are regulated as foods, and not as drugs TRUE	True or False about nutritional supplement (dietary supplement). Nutritional supplements are not pre-approved on their safety and efficacy, unlike drugs TRUE
Lipoprotein is A conjugated protein having a lipid component, the principal means for transporting lipids in the blood	Very low density lipoprotein (VLDL) is A lipoprotein containing a very large proportion of lipids to protein and carrying most cholesterol from the liver to the tissues
Low-density lipoprotein (LDL) is A lipoprotein that contains relatively high amounts of cholesterol and is associated with an increased risk of atherosclerosis and coronary artery disease. It is also called beta-lipoprotein	Chylomicron is Large lipoprotein particle that is created by the absorptive cells of the small intestine. It transports lipids to adipose tissue where they are broken down by lipoprotein lipase
True or False. Hyperlipoproteinemia is a condition marked by an abnormally high level of lipoproteins in the blood. TRUE	True or False. Hypercholesterolemia (or hypercholesteremia) is an abnormally high concentration of cholesterol in the blood. This TRUE
True or False. Familial chylomicronemia (type I) is caused by deficiency in lipoprotein lipase activity. TRUE	True or False. The Coronary Primary Prevention Trial (CPPT) demonstrated that treatment with a lipid-lowering drug could reduce the risk of death due to coronary heart disease. TRUE

True or False. Women taking probucol (Lorelco) should wait for 6 months after cessation of therapy before becoming pregnant. TRUE	True or False. Nicotinic acid (Niacin) plus a bile acid-binding resin has not proven effective in combating hyperlipidemia. FALSE
True or False. Agents, which lower levels of LDL-cholesterol, tend to promote regression of atherosclerotic plaques. TRUE	True or False. Clofibrate (Atromid-S) is the drug of choice for treatment of broad-beta hyperlipidemia (type III). FALSE
True or False. One advantage of gemfibrozil (Lopid) is that, in addition to lowering blood levels of most lipids, it raises the level of HDL cholesterol. TRUE	True or False. Probucol (Lorelco) appears to increase clearance of LDL cholesterol by a non-receptor mediated mechanism. TRUE
True or False about cholestyramine (Questran). It would not be a good choice for treating patients with familial hypertriglyceridemia (type IV) TRUE	True or False about cholestyramine (Questran). It is not well tolerated by patients TRUE
True or False about cholestyramine (Questran). It works by directly binding cholesterol in the blood FALSE	True or False about cholestyramine (Questran). It is an effective drug for treatment of types IIa and IIb hyperlipidemia TRUE

True or False about drugs which inhibit cholesterol synthesis. They work in part by increasing the rate of LDL clearance from the plasma TRUE	True or False about drugs which inhibit cholesterol synthesis. They are the most effective single agents for lowering LDL-cholesterol TRUE
True or False about drugs which inhibit cholesterol synthesis. When used with a bile-acid binding resin, they can lower LDL-cholesterol by 50% or more TRUE	True or False about drugs which inhibit cholesterol synthesis. No special monitoring is required in patients receiving one of them FALSE
True or False about nicotinic acid (Niacin). It reduces the rate of synthesis of VLDL TRUE	True or False about nicotinic acid (Niacin). Sustained-release preparations of this drug are largely free of side effects FALSE
True or False about nicotinic acid (Niacin). Almost all patients taking the traditional dosage form of this drug experience uncomfortable flushing TRUE	True or False about nicotinic acid (Niacin). It should not be used with antihypertensives TRUE
True or False about drugs which inhibit cholesterol synthesis. When used alone, they are the most effective agents for lowering LDL cholesterol TRUE	True or False about drugs which inhibit cholesterol synthesis. They are often effective in patients in whom a diet, with or without a bile acid-binding resin or niacin, has failed TRUE

True or False about drugs which inhibit cholesterol synthesis. Lovastatin (Mevacor) plus a resin causes regression of coronary lesions in about one third of treated patients TRUE	True or False about drugs which inhibit cholesterol synthesis. Members of this drug class are generally not as well tolerated as the older bile acid-binding resins FALSE
True or False about drugs which inhibit cholesterol synthesis. These drugs should not be used in pregnant women or children TRUE	True or False about drugs which inhibit cholesterol synthesis. These drugs often cause myopathy if used in combination with cyclosporine (Sandimmune) TRUE
True or False about drugs which inhibit cholesterol synthesis. Failure to discontinue the drug after myopathy has been detected can cause acute renal failure TRUE	True or False about drugs which inhibit cholesterol synthesis. Several of these drugs tend to lengthen the sleep cycle FALSE
True or False about the fibric acid derivatives. Clofibrate (Atromid-S) is the drug of choice for therapy of Type III hyperlipidemia FALSE	True or False about the fibric acid derivatives. Gemfibrozil (Lopid) increases HDL cholesterol while lowering LDL cholesterol TRUE
True or False about the fibric acid derivatives. Gemfibrozil (Lopid) has been shown to reduce mortality associated with a heart disease TRUE	True or False about the fibric acid derivatives. Gemfibrozil (Lopid) is generally well tolerated TRUE

True or False about the bile acid-binding resins. They decrease total cholesterol and LDL TRUE	True or False about the bile acid-binding resins. They are contraindicated in patients with hypertriglyceridemia TRUE
True or False about the bile acid-binding resins. When used alone, they do not slow the progression of atherosclerotic lesions FALSE	True or False about the bile acid-binding resins. They are the drugs of choice for therapy of type II hyperlipidemia when used either alone or in combination with selected agents TRUE
True or False about nicotinic acid (Niacin). Both triglycerides and LDL cholesterol are reduced by this drug TRUE	True or False about nicotinic acid (Niacin). The drug acts by directly decreasing the rate of synthesis of apoproteins FALSE
True or False about nicotinic acid (Niacin). Doses higher than 3 gm/day are no longer used because of possible disturbances of hepatic or pancreatic functions TRUE	True or False about nicotinic acid (Niacin). Most patients taking this drug experience uncomfortable cutaneous flushing, itching, and/or rashes TRUE
True or False about the general principles of therapy with lipid-lowering drugs. Therapy with a lipid-lowering drug should be always accompanied by an appropriate diet TRUE	True or False about the general principles of therapy with lipid-lowering drugs. Lipid-lowering drugs should only be administered after at least 3 months of prior dietary therapy TRUE

True or False about the general principles of therapy with lipid-lowering drugs. Some combinations of lipid-lowering drugs are synergistic. TRUE	True or False. The cholesterol synthesis inhibitors increase the rate of clearance of LDL cholesterol from the plasma. TRUE
True or False. Lovastatin (Mevacor) plus a bile-acid binding resin causes regression of coronary lesions in about one third of treated patients. TRUE	True or False. The cholesterol synthesis inhibitors are better tolerated than most other lipid-lowering agents. TRUE
True or False. Selected liver and muscle enzymes should be monitored during the use of any cholesterol synthesis inhibitors because of possible toxic effects. TRUE	True or False. The bile acid-binding resins act by directly binding cholesterol and facilitating its excretion. FALSE
True or False. Nicotinic acid (Niacin) acts by increasing the rate of catabolism of VLDL. FALSE	True or False. Gemfibrozil (Lopid) can cause dizziness and syncope when used with antihypertensives. FALSE
True or False. Gemfibrozil (Lopid) increases concentrations of HDL cholesterol more than clofibrate (Atromid-S). TRUE	True or False. The bile acid-binding resins can bind many drugs and vitamins and reduce their absorption. TRUE

True or False. When used alone, the bile acid-binding resins are contraindicated in patients with hypertriglyceridemia. TRUE	True or False. Combinations of lipid-lowering drugs are likely to be synergistic if they work at different steps in the same pathway. TRUE
True or False. Patients with homozygous familial hypercholesterolemia (type IIa) lack any functional LDL receptors on their hepatocytes. TRUE	True or False. Effects of drugs in lowering blood cholesterol levels are additive with those of diet. TRUE
True or False. HMG-CoA reductase inhibiting drugs can cause muscle breakdown, especially when used in combination with a cyclosporine. TRUE	True or False. Probucol (Lorelco) reduces the risk of atherosclerosis by stimulating the rate of clearance of LDL by receptor-mediated pathways. FALSE
True or False. Clofibrate (Atromid-S) is generally regarded as superior to gemfibrozil. FALSE	True or False. Niacin's most common side effects can be reduced by pretreatment with aspirin and/or by taking the drug at the end of meals. TRUE
True or False. The major side effect of cholestyramine is hepatotoxicity. FALSE	True or False. The statins are dependent on the presence of LDL receptors on hepatocytes in order to exert their effect. FALSE

This drug increases lipoprotein lipase (LPL) activity in adipose tissue Gemfibrozil (Loprol)	This drug both inhibits an enzyme and indirectly enhances clearance of low density lipoproteins (LDL) Lovastatin (Mevacor)
This drug binds bile acids in the GI tract Cholestyramine (Questran)	This drug may block oxidation of low density lipoproteins (LDL) Probucol (Lorelco)
This drug weakly stimulates synthesis of very low density lipoproteins (VLDL) Cholestyramine (Questran)	Flushing caused by this drug can be reduced by taking it after meals and/or by pretreatment with aspirin Nicotinic acid (niacin)
This drug can cause muscle damage, especially when used with any of several drugs including erythromycin Lovastatin (Mevacor)	This drug decreases blood levels of high density lipoproteins (HDL) Probucol (Lorelco)
This fibric acid derivative increases blood levels of high density lipoproteins (HDL): Gemfibrozil (Loprol)	True or False. Gout is a familial metabolic disease characterized by recurrent episodes of acute arthritis due to deposits of monosodium urate in joints and cartilage. TRUE

Which drugs is an uricosuric agent Sulfinpyrazone	**Uricosuric drugs are** - Probenecid - Sulfinpyrazone - Aspirin (at high dosages)
Which drugs used in the treatment of gout acts by preventing the migration of granulocytes Colchicine	**Which drugs used in the treatment of gout has as its primary effect the reduction of uric acid synthesis** Allopurinol
Characteristics of probenecid include - It is useful in the treatment of gout - At appropriate doses, it promotes the excretion of uric acid - The metabolic products of probenecid are uricosuric	**True or False. The parathyroid hormone increases serum calcium and decreases serum phosphate.** TRUE
True or False about parathyroid hormone. The parathyroid hormone (PTH) is a single-chain peptide hormone composed of 84 amino acids TRUE	**True or False about parathyroid hormone. The parathyroid hormone increases calcium and phosphate absorption in intestine (by increased 1,25-dihydroxyvitamin D3 production)** TRUE
True or False about parathyroid hormone. The parathyroid hormone increases serum calcium and decreases serum phosphate TRUE	**True or False about parathyroid hormone. The parathyroid hormone increases calcium excretion and decreases phosphate excretion in kidneys** FALSE

True or False about calcitonin. Calcitonin secreted by parafollicular cells of the mammalian thyroid is a single-chain peptide hormone with 32 amino acids TRUE	**True or False about calcitonin.** Effects of calcitonin are to lower serum calcium and phosphate by acting on bones and kidneys. TRUE
True or False about calcitonin. Calcitonin inhibits osteoclastic bone resorption. TRUE	**Mechanism of action of calcitonin is** Raises intracellular cAMP in osteoclasts
Indications for calcitonin administration are - Hypercalcemia - Paget's disease - Osteoporosis	**Side effect of calcitonin is** Tetany
Side effect of calcitonin is Hypotension	**Glucocorticoid hormones alter bone mineral homeostasis** - By antagonizing vitamin D-stimulated intestinal calcium transport - By stimulating renal calcium excretion - By increasing parathyroid hormone stimulated bone resorption
True or False. Estrogens can prevent accelerated bone loss during the immediate postmenopausal period and at least transiently increase bone in the postmenopausal subject. TRUE	**True or False.** Vitamin D3 increases serum calcium and phosphate. TRUE

Route of administration of vitamin D3 is Oral	Side effect of vitamin D3 is Nephrolithiasis
Indication of vitamin D3 is Hypophosphatemia	Route of administration of 25-hydroxyvitamin D3 (calcifediol) is Oral
Indication for 25-hydroxyvitamin D3 (calcifediol) administration is Failure of vitamin D formation in skin	Side effect of 25-hydroxyvitamin D3 (calcifediol) is - Hypercalcemia- Pruritus- GI toxicity
Indications for 1,25-dihydroxyvitamin D3 (calcitriol) administration are - Hypocalcemia in chronic renal failure- Vitamin D-dependent rickets- Malabsorption of vitamin D from intestine	Indication for 1,25-dihydroxyvitamin D3 (calcitriol) administration is Hypophosphatemia
True or False about 1,25-dihydroxyvitamin D3 (calcitriol). Calcitriol also raises serum phosphate, though this action is usually not observed early in treatment TRUE	True or False about 1,25-dihydroxyvitamin D3 (calcitriol). Undergoes enterohepatic circulation TRUE

Route of administration of 1,25-dihydroxyvitamin D3 (calcitriol) is Oral	Commercially available analogs of 1,25-dihydroxyvitamin D3 (calcitriol) are - Doxercalciferol (Hectoral)- Paricalcitol (Zemplar)
Side effect of dihydrotachysterol is Hypertension	Route of administration of dihydrotachysterol is Oral
Which statements refers to cholecalciferol Mechanism of action: 1. Genomic effects 2. Cytoplasmic effects	Indication for cholecalciferol administration is Malabsorption of vitamin D from intestine
Route of administration of cholecalciferol is Oral	The unwanted effect of cholecalciferol is CNS toxicity
The unwanted effect of dihydrotachysterol is CNS toxicity	Indication for dihydrotachysterol administration is Hypophosphatemia

Conditions associated with hypophosphatemia include - Primary hyperparathyroidism- Vitamin D deficiency- Idiopathic hypercalciuria	True or False. The long-term effects of hypophosphatemia include proximal muscle weakness and abnormal bone mineralization (osteomalacia). TRUE
Recommended phosphorus daily allowance is 900-1200 mg	Interactions with other drugs of phosphorus is Calcitonin: increases renal excretion
Indication for pamidronate administration is Hypercalcemia	Route of administration of pamidronate is Intravenous
True or False about pamidronate include. Because it causes gastric irritation, pamidronate is not available as an oral preparation TRUE	True or False about pamidronate include. Skeletal half-life is 24 h FALSE
True or False about pamidronate include. Fever and lymphocytopenia are reversible TRUE	True or False about pamidronate include. Can be irritable to the esophagus if not washed promptly to the stomach TRUE

Route of administration of alendronate is Oral	True or False about alendronate include. Can be irritable to the esophagus if not washed promptly to the stomach TRUE
True or False about alendronate include. 1st generation biphosphonate FALSE	True or False about alendronate include. Reduces osteoclast activity without significantly affecting osteoblasts, useful in the treatment of Paget's disease TRUE
True or False about alendronate include. More potent than EHDP, has a wider therapeutic window TRUE	Indications of alendronate are - Glucocorticoid-induced osteoporosis- Paget's disease- Syndromes of ectopic calcification
Indication for etidronate administration is Paget's disease	Indications for etidronate administration are - Paget's disease- Osteoporosis- Hypercalcemia
True or False about etidronate. Bioavailability increases with the administered dose TRUE	True or False about etidronate include. Skeletal half-life is hundreds of days TRUE

True or False about etidronate include. Bioavailability increases with the administered dose TRUE	True or False about etidronate include. 2nd generation biphosphonate (amino-biphosphonate) FALSE
True or False about etidronate include. 1st generation biphosphonate. TRUE	Unwanted effect of etidronate is: Defective bone mineralization
The major causes of hypocalcemia in the adult are - Hypoparathyroidism- Vitamin D deficiency- Renal failure and malabsorption	The major causes of hypercalcemia in the adult are - Hyperparathyroidism- Cancer with or without bone metastases- Hypervitaminosis D
True or False about calcium. Recommended Ca daily allowance for males: 1. 1-10 years: 800 mg 2. 11-18 years: 1200 mg 3. 19-50 years: 1000 mg 4. > 51 years: 1000 mg TRUE	True or False about calcium. Ca chloride is very irritating and can cause necrosis if extravasated TRUE
Indication for calcium administration is Vitamin D deficiency	Which of the calcium preparations is the most preferable for IV injection Calcium gluconate (0.45 meq calcium/mL)

Which of the oral calcium preparations is often the preparation of choice Calcium carbonate (40% calcium)	**Interactions with other drugs of calcium is** - Ethanol: decreases absorption - Loop diuretics: increase renal excretion - Glucocorticoids: stimulate renal excretion
True or False about magnesium include. Magnesium is mainly an intracellular cation, and is the fourth most abundant cation in the body TRUE	**True or False about magnesium include. The recommended dietary amounts of magnesium have been set at 6 mg/kg day (350-400 mg)** TRUE
True or False about magnesium include. It is a physiological calcium agonist FALSE	**Recommended magnesium daily allowance is** 350-400 mg
Which of the magnesium preparation is the most preferable for I.V. injection Magnesium chloride	**Which of the oral magnesium preparations is often the preparation of choice** MagneB6 (Mg pidolate / Mg lactate + pyridoxine hydrochloride)
True or False about fluoride include. Fluoride is effective for the prophylaxis of dental caries TRUE	**True or False about fluoride include. Fluoride is accumulated by bone and teeth, where it may stabilize the hydroxyapatite crystal** TRUE

Recommended fluoride daily allowance is 1.5-4 mg	True or False about gallium nitrate. It is approved by the FDA for the management of hypercalcemia of malignancy TRUE
True or False about gallium nitrate. This drug acts by inhibiting bone resorption TRUE	True or False about gallium nitrate. Because of potential nephrotoxicity, patients should be well-hydrated and have good renal output before starting the infusion TRUE
True or False about plicamycin (formerly mithramycin). Duration of action is usually several days TRUE	True or False about plicamycin (formerly mithramycin). Mechanism of cytotoxic action appears to involve its binding to DNA, possibly through an antibiotic-Mg2+ complex. TRUE
Unwanted effects of plicamycin (formerly mithramycin) are Fractures	Unwanted effect of plicamycin (formerly mithramycin) is Myelosuppression
Indication for plicamycin (formerly mithramycin) administration is - Testicular cancers refractory to standard treatment- Paget's disease- Hypercalcemia of malignancy	Route of administration of plicamycin is Intravenous

Mineralocorticoid effects cause Increased Na retension and K excretion	**Which synthetic steroids shows predominantly mineralocorticoid action?** Fludrocortisone
The major mineralocorticoids are Hydrocortisone	**True or False about spironolactone. Spironolactone reverses many of the manifestations of aldosteronism** TRUE
True or False about spironolactone. Spironilactone is also an androgen antagonist and as such is used in the treatment of hirsutism in wormen TRUE	**True or False about spironolactone. Spironolactone is useful as a diuretic** TRUE
True or False about diuretics. Carbonic anhydrase inhibition leads to increased reabsorption of NaHCO3 FALSE	**True or False about diuretics. Loop diuretics decrease Na+ reabsorption at the loop of Henle by competing for the Cl- site on the Na+/K+/2Cl cotransporter** TRUE
True or False about diuretics. In general, the potency of a diuretic is determined by where it acts in the renal tubule TRUE	**True or False about diuretics. Hydrochlorothiazide decreases urinary calcium excretion** TRUE

The drug inhibits the ubiquitous enzyme carbonic anhydrase Acetazolamide (Diamox)	The drug acts by competitively blocking NaCl cotransporters in the distal tubule Hydrochlorothiazide (HydroDiuril)
The drug acts at the proximal tubule Acetazolamide (Diamox)	The drug acts by competing with aldosterone for its cytosolic receptors Spironolactone (Aldactone)
The drug is a potassium-sparing diuretic that blocks Na+ channels in the collecting tubules Amiloride (Midamor)	Chronic use of this drug can lead to distal tubular hypertrophy, which may reduce its diuretic effect Furosemide (Lasix)
The drug has a steroid-like structure which is responsible for its anti-androgenic effect Spironolactone (Aldactone)	Sustained use of this drug results in increased plasma urate concentrations Furosemide (Lasix)
The drug can be used to treat glaucoma Acetazolamide (Diamox)	The drug can cause ototoxicity Furosemide (Lasix)

The drug acts only on the lumenal side of renal tubules Furosemide (Lasix)	The drug can promote sodium loss in patients with low (e.g., 40 ml/min) glomerular filtration rates Furosemide (Lasix)
The drug can be used to treat nephrogenic diabetes insipidus Hydrochlorothiazide (HydroDiuril)	The drug is sometimes part of fixed-dose combinations used to treat essential hypertension - Hydrochlorothiazide (HydroDiuril)- Amiloride (Midamor)
The drug should never be administered to patients taking potassium supplements Amiloride (Midamor)	The drug decreases calcium excretion in urine Hydrochlorothiazide (HydroDiuril)
The drug acts by competitively blocking the Na+/K+/2Cl- cotransporter Loop diuretics	The drug acts at the proximal tubule Carbonic anhydrase inhibitors
The drug acts in the distal convoluted tubule Thiazide diuretics	The drug acts in the collecting tubules Potassium-sparing diuretics

The drug is the most potent diuretic Loop diuretics	The drug acts by competitively blocking the NaCl cotransporter Thiazide diuretics
The drug inhibits sodium and chloride transport in the cortical thick ascending limb and the early distal tubule Hydrochlorothiazide (Hydrodiuril)	The drug can cause ototoxicity Furosemide (Lasix)
The drug blocks the sodium/potassium/chloride cotransporter in the thick ascending loop of Henle Furosemide (Lasix)	The drug is one of the most potent diuretics Furosemide (Lasix)
The drug is usually given in combination with a thiazide diuretic Amiloride (Midamor)	True or False about diuretics. Furosemide (Lasix) can increase the likelihood of digitalis toxicity TRUE
True or False about diuretics. Chlorthalidone (Hygroton) can decrease the excretion of lithium TRUE	True or False about diuretics. Ibuprofen can increase the antihypertensive effect of chlorthalidone FALSE

True or False about diuretics. Chlorthalidone has a longer duration of action than furosemide TRUE	The drug is the least potent diuretic Potassium-sparing diuretics
These agents must be given parenterally because they are not absorbed when given orally Osmotic diuretics	These drugs may be used in the treatment of recurrent calcium nephrolithiasis Loop diuretics
Furosemide (Lasix) acts at this nephron site Ascending thick limb of the loop of Henle	Metolazone (Mykrox) acts at this nephron site Distal convoluted tubule
Acetazolamide (Diamox) acts at this nephron site Proximal convoluted tubule	Spironolactone (Aldactone) acts at this nephron site Collecting duct
Amiloride (Midamone) acts at this nephron site Collecting duct	The drug competitively blocks chloride channels and prevents movement of sodium, potassium, and chloride into the renal tubular cells Furosemide (Lasix)

The drug acts by affecting the tubular fluid composition in a non-receptor mediated fashion Mannitol (Osmitrol)	The drug is a blood substitute having haemodynamical activity Polyglucinum
This drug is a desintoxicative plasma substitute Haemodesum	This drug is a controller of water-salt and acid-basic state "Disolum", "Trisolum"
What does the term "antibiotics" mean Substances produced by some microorganisms and their synthetic analogues that selectively kill or inhibit the growth of another microorganisms	Minimal duration of antibacterial treatment usually is Not less than 5 days
Rational anti-microbial combination is used to - Provide synergism when microorganisms are not effectively eradicated with a single agent alone- Provide broad coverage- Prevent the emergence of resistance	Mechanisms of bacterial resistance to anti-microbial agents are - Active transport out of a microorganism or/and hydrolysis of an agent via enzymes produced by a microorganism- Modification of a drug's target- Reduced uptake by a microorganism
True or False. The statement, that some microorganisms can develop alternative metabolic pathways for rendering reactions inhibited by the drug TRUE	Bactericidal effect is Destroying of bacterial cells

Which roups of antibiotics demonstrates a bactericidal effect?	Penicillins
Bacteristatic effect is	Inhibition of bacterial cell division
Which groups of antibiotics demonstrates a bacteristatic effect	Macrolides
Which antibiotics contains a beta-lactam ring in their chemical structure	- Penicillins- Cephalosporins- Carbapenems and monobactams
Drug belonging to antibiotics-macrolides	Erythromycin
Drug belonging to antibiotics-carbapenems	Imipinem
Drug belonging to antibiotics-monobactams	Aztreonam
Drug belongs to antibiotics-cephalosporins	Cefaclor
Drug belonging to lincozamides	Lincomycin
Drug belonging to antibiotics-tetracyclines	Doxycycline

Examples of aminoglycosides - Gentamycin - Streptomycin - Neomycin	**Drug belonging to nitrobenzene derivative** Chloramphenicol
Drug belonging to glycopeptides Vancomycin	**Antibiotics inhibiting the bacterial cell wall synthesis are** Beta-lactam antibiotics
Antibiotic inhibiting bacterial RNA synthesis is Rifampin	**Antibiotics altering permeability of cell membranes are** Polymyxins
All of the following antibiotics inhibit the protein synthesis in bacterial cells - Macrolides - Aminoglycosides - Tetracyclines	**Biosynthetic penicillins are effective against** Gram-positive and gram-negative cocci, Corynebacterium diphtheria, spirochetes, Clostridium gangrene
Which drugs is a gastric acid resistant Penicillin V	**Which drugs is penicillinase resistant** Oxacillin

All of the following drugs demonstrate a prolonged effect - Procain penicillin - Bicillin-1 - Bicillin-5	**Mechanism of penicillins' antibacterial effect is** Inhibition of transpeptidation in the bacterial cell wall
Beta-lactamase inhibitor for co-administration with penicillins - Clavulanic acid - Sulbactam - Tazobactam	**Cephalosporines are drugs of choice for treatment of** Gram-negative and gram-positive microorganism infections, if penicillins have no effect
Carbapenems are effective against Broad-spectrum	**All of the following antibiotics are macrolides** - Erythromycin - Clarithromycin - Roxythromycin
Tetracyclins have following unwanted effects - Irritation of gastrointestinal mucosa, phototoxicity - Hepatotoxicity, anti-anabolic effect - Dental hypoplasia, bone deformities	**Drug belonging to antibiotics-aminoglycosides** Gentamycin
Aminoglycosides are effective against Broad-spectrum, except anaerobic microorganisms and viruses	**Aminoglycosides have the following unwanted effects** Ototoxicity, nephrotoxicity

Characteristics of chloramphenicol	Chloramphenicol has the following unwanted effects
Broad-spectum. Demonstrates a bactericidal effect.	Pancytopenia
Characteristics of lincozamides	Lincozamides have the following unwanted effect
Influence mainly the anaerobic organisms, Gram positive cocci.	Pseudomembranous colitis
Characteristics of vancomicin	Vancomicin has the following unwanted effects
It is a glycopeptide, inhibits cell wall synthesis and is active only against Gram-positive bacteria.	"Red neck" syndrome, phlebitis
Which drugs is used for systemic and deep mycotic infections treatment:	Which drugs is used for dermatomycosis treatment
Amphotericin B	Griseofulvin
Which drugs is used for candidiasis treatment	The following antifungal drugs are antibiotics
Myconazol	Myconazol

Mechanism of Amphotericin B action is Alteration of cell membrane permeability	**Azoles have an antifungal effect because of** Reduction of ergosterol synthesis
Which drugs alters permeability of Candida cell membranes Nystatin	**Amfotericin B has the following unwanted effects** Renal impairment, anemia
Drug belonging to antibiotics having a polyene structure Nystatin	**The following drugs demonstrate a fungicidal effect** - Terbinafin- Ketoconazole- Myconazol
The following drug do not demonstrate a fungicidal effect Amfotericin B	**Characteristics of polyenes are** - Alter the structure and functions of cell membranes- Broad-spectrum- Nephrotoxicity, hepatotoxicity
Characteristics of polyenes are not Fungicidal effect	**Characteristics of Amfotericin B are** - Used for systemic mycosis treatment- Poor absorption from the gastro-intestinal tract- Influences the permeability of fungus cell membrane

Characteristics of Amfotericin B are not Does not demonstrate nephrotoxicity	**Sulfonamides are effective against** - Bacteria and Chlamidia- Actinomyces- Protozoa
Mechanism of sulfonamides' antibacterial effect is Inhibition of dihydropteroate synthase	**Combination of sulfonamides with trimethoprim** Increases the antimicrobial activity
Sulfonamide potency is decreased in case of co-administration with Local anesthetics – derivatives of paraaminobenzoic acid	**The following measures are necessary for prevention of sulfonamide precipitation and crystalluria** Taking of drinks with alkaline pH
Resorptive sulfonamides have the following unwanted effects on blood system - Hemolytic anemia- Thrombocytopenia- Granulocytopenia	**Mechanism of Trimethoprim' action is** Inhibition of dihydropteroate reductase
Sulfonamides have the following unwanted effects - Hematopoietic disturbances- Crystalluria- Nausea, vomiting and diarrhea	**The drug, which is effective against mycobacteria only** Isoniazid

The antimycobacterial drug belonging to first-line agents Isoniazid	The antimycobacterial drug, belonging to second-line agents PAS
The antimycobacterial drug, belonging to antibiotics Rifampin	Mechanism of Izoniazid action is Inhibition of mycolic acids synthesis
Mechanism of Rifampin action is Inhibition of DNA dependent RNA polymerase	Mechanism of Cycloserine action is Inhibition of cell wall synthesis
Mechanism of Streptomycin action is Inhibition of protein synthesis	Rifampin has the following unwanted effect Flu-like syndrome, tubular necrosis
Isoniazid has following unwanted effect Hepatotoxicity, peripheral neuropathy	Ethambutol has the following unwanted effect Retrobulbar neuritis with red-green color blindness

Streptomycin has the following unwanted effect Ototoxicity, nephrotoxicity	**Mechanism of aminosalicylic acid action is** Inhibition of folate synthesis
The following agents are the first-line antimycobacterial drugs - Rifampin - Isoniazid - Streptomycin	**The following antimycobacterial drugs have a bactericidal effect** - Streptomycin - Rifampin - Isoniazid
Combined chemotherapy of tuberculosis is used to Decrease mycobacterium drug-resistance	**Antibacterial drug – a nitrofurane derivative** Nitrofurantoin
Antibacterial drug – a nitroimidazole derivative Metronidazole	**Antibacterial drug – a quinolone derivative** Nalidixic acid
Antibacterial drug – a fluoroquinolone derivative Ciprofloxacin	**The indications for nitrofuranes** Infections of urinary and gastro-intestinal tracts

The unwanted effects of nitrofuranes - Nausea, vomiting- Allergic reactions- Hemolytic anemia	**The indications for Metronidazole** Intra-abdominal infections, vaginitis, enterocolitis
The unwanted effects of Metronidazole Nausea, vomiting, diarrhea, stomatitis	**The mechanism of fluoroquinolones' action is** Inhibition of DNA gyrase
Fluoroquinolones are active against Variety of Gram-negative and positive microorganisms, including Mycoplasmas and Chlamidiae	**The unwanted effects of fluoroquinolones** Headache, dizziness, insomnia
The indications for fluoroquinolones Infections of the urinary and respiratory tract, bacterial diarrhea	**The drug of choice for syphilis treatment is** Penicillin
The drug used for malaria chemoprophylaxis and treatment Chloroquine	**The drug used for amoebiasis treatment** Iodoquinol

The drug used for trichomoniasis treatment Metronidazole	The drug used for toxoplasmosis treatment Pyrimethamine
The drug used for balantidiasis treatment Tetracycline	The drug used for leishmaniasis treatment Sodium stibogluconate
The antimalarial drug belonging to 8-aminoquinoline derivatives Primaquine	The following antimalarial drugs are 4-quinoline derivatives - Chloroquine - Mefloquine - Amodiaquine
The following antimalarial drugs are not 4-quinoline derivatives Primaquine	The antimalarial drug belonging to pyrimidine derivat Pyrimethamine
The drug used for trypanosomosis treatment Melarsoprol	The antimalarial drug having a gametocidal effect Primaquine

The following antimalarial drugs influence blood schizonts - Mefloquine- Chloroquine- Quinidine	The following antimalarial drugs do not influence blood schizonts Primaquine
The antimalarial drug influencing tissue schisonts Primaquine	The group of antibiotics having an antimalarial effect Tetracyclins
The amebecide drug for the treatment of an asymptomatic intestinal form of amebiasis Diloxanide	The drugs for the treatment of an intestinal form of amebiasis Metronidazole and diloxanide
The drug for the treatment of a hepatic form of amebiasis Metronidazole or emetine	The luminal amebecide drug Diloxanide
The drug of choice for the treatment of extraluminal amebiasis Metronidazole	The drug, blocking acetylcholine transmission at the myoneural junction of helminthes Piperazine

Niclosamide mechanism of action Inhibiting oxidative phosphorylation in some species of helminthes	**Praziquantel mechanism of action** Increasing cell membrane permeability for calcium, resulting in paralysis, dislodgement and death of helminthes
Piperazine mechanism of action Blocking acetylcholine transmission at the myoneural junction and paralysis of helminthes	The drug, a salicylamide derivative Niclosamide
Mebendazole mechanism of action Inhibiting microtubule synthesis in helminthes and irreversible impairment of glucose uptake	The drug, inhibiting oxidative phosphorylation in some species of helminthes Niclosamide
The drug for neurocysticercosis treatment Praziquante	The drug for nematodosis (roundworm invasion) treatment Pyrantel
The drug for cestodosis (tapeworm invasion) treatment Praziquantel	The drug for trematodosis (fluke invasion) treatment Bithionol

The drug, a benzimidazole derivative Mebendazole	The broad spectrum drug for cestodosis, trematodosis and cycticercosis treatment Praziquantel
The drug for ascaridosis and enterobiosis treatment Pyrantel	The drug for strongiloidosis treatment Ivermectin
The drug for echinococcosis treatment Mebendazole or Albendazole	The following antiviral drugs are the analogs of nucleosides Saquinavir
The drug, a derivative of adamantane Rimantadine	The drug, a derivative of pyrophosphate Foscarnet
The drug, inhibiting viral DNA synthesis Acyclovir	The drug, inhibiting uncoating of the viral RNA Rimantadine

The drug, inhibiting viral reverse transcriptase Zidovudine	The drug, inhibiting viral proteases Saquinavir
The drug of choice for herpes and cytomegalovirus infection treatment Acyclovir	The drug which belongs to nonnucleoside reverse transcriptase inhibitors Nevirapine
The following antiviral drugs are antiretroviral agents - Zidovudine - Zalcitabine - Didanozine	The drug used for influenza A prevention Rimantadine
The drug used for HIV infection treatment, a derivative of nucleosides Zidovudine	The antiviral drug which belongs to endogenous proteins Interferon alfa
The drug which belongs to nucleoside reverse transcriptase inhibitors Didanosine	The following antiviral drugs are anti-influenza agents - Amantadine - Interferons - Rimantadine

The unwanted effects of zidovudine Anemia, neutropenia, nausea, insomnia	**The unwanted effects of intravenous acyclovir infusion** Renal insufficiency, tremors, delerium
The drug that can induce peripheral neuropathy and oral ulceration Zalcitabine	**The unwanted effects of didanozine** Peripheral neuropathy, pancreatitis, diarrhea, hyperuricemia
The unwanted effects of indinavir Nephrolithiasis, nausea, hepatotoxicity	**The drug that can induce nausea, diarrhea, abdominal pain and rhinitis** Saquinavir
The following effects are disadvantages of anticancer drugs - Low selectivity to cancer cells- Depression of bone marrow- Depression of immune system	**Rational combination of anticancer drugs is used to** Provide synergism resulting from the use of anticancer drugs with different mechanisms combination
The anticancer alkylating drug, a derivative of chloroethylamine Cyclophosphamide	**The anticancer alkylating drug, a derivative of ethylenimine** Thiotepa

The group of hormonal drugs used for cancer treatment Glucocorticoids and gonadal hormones	**The anticancer alkylating drug, a derivative of alkylsulfonate** Busulfan
The anticancer drug of plant origin Vincristine	**Action mechanism of alkylating agents is** Producing carbonium ions altering DNA structure
The anticancer drug, a pyrimidine antagonist Fluorouracil	**Methotrexate is** A folic acid antagonist
The antibiotic for cancer chemotherapy Doxorubicin	**Fluorouracil belongs to** Antimetabolites
The action mechanism of anticancer drugs belonging to plant alkaloids Mitotic arrest at a metaphase	**General contraindications for anticancer drugs are** - Depression of bone marrow - Acute infections - Severe hepatic and/or renal insufficiency

Action mechanism of methotrexate is Inhibition of dihydrofolate reductase	**The anticancer drug belonging to inorganic metal complexes** Cisplatin
The indication for estrogens in oncological practice Cancer of prostate	**Enzyme drug used for acute leukemia treatment** Dihydrofolate reductase
The following drugs are derivatives of nitrosoureas - Carmustine - Lomustine - Semustine	**The group of drugs used as subsidiary medicines in cancer treatment** - Cytoprotectors - Bone marrow growth factors - Antimetastatic agents
Estrogen inhibitor Tamoxifen	**Antiandrogen drug** Flutamide
The drug belonging to aromatase inhibitors Anastrozole	**The drug belonging to gonadotropin-releasing hormone agonists** Leuprolide